D0772466

Politics and Religion during the English Revolution

The publication of this work has
been aided by a grant from the
Andrew W. Mellon Foundation

Politics and Religion during the English Revolution

The Scots and the Long Parliament 1643–1645

Lawrence Kaplan

New York: New York University Press · 1976

Library of Congress Catalog Card Number: 76-13255
ISBN: 0-8147-4563-6

Library of Congress Cataloging in Publication Data
Kaplan, Lawrence.
Politics and religion during the English Revolution.

Bibliography: p.
Includes index.
1. Great Britain–Politics and government–1642-1649. 2. Scotland–Politics and government–1625-1649. 3. Covenanters. I. Title.
DA415.K36 322′.1′0941 76-13255
ISBN 0-8147-4563-6

Manufactured in the United States of America

For the memory of Ellen Sparer Bindman

Preface

In recent years there has been a renewed interest in the political history of Civil War England, a subject which had remained relatively dormant following S. R. Gardiner's multivolume account of the early seventeenth century. Since J. H. Hexter published his brilliant analysis of John Pym in 1941 it has become obvious that Gardiner's narrative, however impressive, was sorely in need of revision. Several books and articles of varying quality, dealing with the politics of the Long Parliament, have lately appeared and it is the intention of this present study to add to a growing literature.

The topic of the Covenanters' involvement in England suggested itself for further investigation because the key role played by the Scots in the English Civil War has frequently been mentioned, but never has it been studied in depth. The purpose of this book is both to describe and to analyze the interrelationships of the Covenanters and the English Parliament between 1643 and 1645, in order to treat a neglected subject and also to provide a somewhat different emphasis to political and religious matters than is usually given. It is hoped that this vantage point will allow the reexamination of long-held views and, in some instances, suggest new interpretations.

The great revolutions of the past have tended to pass through stages as they moved in a generally leftward drift. The period analyzed in this book (1643–1645) represents a particular stage in the progression of the English Revolution. The intervention of the Scots helped radicalize the conflict, while the development of the New Model Army as the dominant military force in the land after 1645 indicated that a new stage had been reached.

In the preparation of this book I have received assistance and encouragement from teachers, colleagues, and friends. My debt to J. H. Hexter of Yale University is unending. His sharp sense of logic has proven to be of enormous value. In addition, I have benefited immensely from Professor Hexter's own writings, not the least of which was his unpublished thesis, "The Rise of the Independent Party," Harvard University, 1936.

The following scholars have been generous with their time and suggestions over the years: Professor Tai Liu, Mr. Walter Makey, Dr. Valerie Pearl, Professor H. R. Trevor-Roper, Professor David Underdown, and Dame Veronica Wedgwood. However, I alone am responsible for the conclusions in this book. My good friend Mrs. Gladys Hartman kindly typed the manuscript.

I must also extend my appreciation to the following institutions for allowing me to continue my research and writing over three summers: the William Andrews Clark Library of U.C.L.A., the American Philosophical Society, and the City University Faculty Research Award.

Sections of this present book first appeared in somewhat different form in *Church History* and the *Journal of British Studies*: and I wish to thank the editors of these journals for permission to reprint this material.

My greatest debt is to my wife, Carol, to whom everything is owed.

Englewood, New Jersey
September, 1975

Contents

Introduction

In enumerating the principal direct causes of the English Revolution historians inevitably call attention to the failure of royal policy in Scotland. For as part of his strategy of drawing all his dominions under increased control Charles I, counseled by Archbishop Laud, decided to force Scotland into greater conformity with the more subservient episcopacy of England. By extending English ecclesiastical practices, the king hoped to undermine the wealth and independence of both the kirk and the Scottish aristocracy, who benefited from the existing situation. But this decision to expand his power in the northern kingdom proved to be his undoing.

The resistance to the new English Prayer Book that began in Edinburgh during July 1637 quickly spread. Before long practically the whole country had joined together to oppose the king. The religious issue became the bond which unified all of Scotland, and as long as their religion was under fire most influential Scotsmen supported the opposition to the Crown. By February 1638 leaders of the kirk and the nobility drew up a National Covenant which united the nation against those who wished to introduce innovations into "the true Christian faith and religion."[1] The General Assembly of the kirk, meeting in November 1638, disobeyed the king's order to dissolve, and by the time its proceedings came to an end the covenanters had declared episcopacy abolished. These overt acts of defiance, revolutionary in their nature, brought on a war between the two kingdoms–a war which Charles could not afford either politically or financially.[2]

Humiliated in the First Bishops' War of June 1639, the king summoned his English Parliament to help finance further military action against the Scots. Parliament, however, refused to grant funds until their grievances had been redressed–a quid pro quo that Charles found unacceptable, and he therefore dissolved the two houses in short order. When the Second Bishops' War proved even more difficult to terminate than the first, the king was compelled to recall, in November 1640, a Parliament that demanded retribution for "eleven years of tyranny." Less than two years later the impasse between Crown and Parliament, never solved, resulted in a civil war between the two. Charles's decision to alter the religious situation in Scotland had set off a chain of events which led to catastrophe.

The Scottish revolt did not remain an exclusively religious one: what started as a protest against ecclesiastical innovations became increasingly political. By excluding bishops from the Estates, as they did in June 1640, the Scots considerably weakened the power of the king in their Parliament. The royal prerogative was also reduced by the demand of the Scottish Parliament that it should be consulted whenever the king desired to make appointments of officers of state, privy councillors, and judges. In addition, a triennial act was passed ensuring that Parliament would meet every three years, while a permanent Committee of the Estates would exercise authority when it was not in session.[3]

This state of legislation, S. R. Gardiner tells us, "implied that Parliament and not the King was to be the central force in Scotland."[4] It transformed political institutions even more dramatically than religious ones, as contemporaries realized. Sir James Balfour, the chronicler of the Scottish Parliament, described the legislation as

> the real greatest change at one blow that ever happened to this church and state these 600 years by past; for in effect it overturned not only

> the ancient state government, but fettered monarchy with chains, and set new limits and marks to the same, beyond which it was not legal to proceed.[5]

As the English assault on Presbyterianism diminished and then finally expired, the solidarity achieved between 1637 and 1640 expired also. Certain Scottish nobles who had been willing to rise to the defense of their national religion did not want the Estates to go over to the offensive in reducing the king's authority. This latter group, led by the Earl of Montrose, had in August 1640 drawn up the Cumbernauld Bond, establishing the signatories' loyalty to Crown and Covenant against what they regarded as the pretensions of ambitious men.[6] Thus the Covenanting Party began to dissolve as political issues became uppermost. In the period 1640-1643 (that is, from the end of the Second Bishops' War until the Scots intervened in the English Civil War) one can observe the emergence of different political factions within Scotland.

Despite the growing political character of the Scottish Revolution, the kirk continued to exercise considerable influence in affairs of state. It was one thing to prevent the king from interfering in church matters; it was quite another for the king to keep the kirk out of politics. Indeed, the church in Scotland held that the civil authorities should be reminded of their Christian duties regularly. They believed firmly that the state ought to be kept subordinate to the church,[7] and the General Assembly never hesitated to direct Scottish leaders along the path of righteousness. Because of their enormous influence the kirk wielded much secular power.

As soon as actual fighting commenced in England during the summer of 1642, the kirk assumed a definite stance in favor of joining the war on Parliament's side. Undoubtedly zealots like Lord Wariston, a ruling elder of the church, saw the conflict as a God-given opportunity to advance the cause of Presbyterianism by force of arms.[8] But the question of self-preservation existed as well. Even rather restrained members of the kirk dreaded a Royalist victory over Parliament, which would leave Charles with a free hand to settle his previous score with Scotland. Scottish Presbyterians believed that they could never be safe until expansionist Anglicanism was dethroned in England.[9]

Working in collaboration with the church to bring about an alliance with the Long Parliament was Archibald Campbell, the Marquis of Argyll, who some considered to be "the most powerful subject in the kingdom." [10] The political changes of the previous years had enhanced Argyll's stature as well as that of certain other Scottish nobles like Chancellor Loudoun and Baron Balmerino, and at the same time had given the lairds a greater voice in the political process. These groups had a vested interest in the perpetuation of a weak monarchy and thus, together with the leaders of the kirk, they openly sided with the English Parliament from the beginning of the conflict.

The main opposition to the church party came from a segment of the upper class which followed the leadership of James, Duke of Hamilton, the king's special adviser on Scotland. Despite some unfortunate experiences with his services in the past, the king continued to hold Hamilton in high regard, and the fact that he represented Charles caused many nobles to attach themselves to him "for considerations of interest." [11] Deriving his principal support from a large network of influential relatives such as his brother, the Earl of Lanark, the secretary of state for Scotland, and officeholders like the king's treasurer, the Earl of Traquair, Hamilton picked up further followers from among those nobles who resented Argyll's position of supremacy.[12]

Surely the Hamilton party favored a Royalist victory in England; yet given the lack of sympathy for Charles that prevailed in the country, these moderates never seriously contemplated bringing Scottish troops into the Civil War on the side of the Crown. They merely wanted to keep Scotland neutral so that the Royalists could defeat their enemy without any interference, so confident were they of the outcome.[13] Hamilton's task was made easier by the presence in Edinburgh of numerous aristocrats who refused to join either the Hamilton or the Argyll faction, but who nevertheless agreed with the former that Scotland would best be served by remaining out of an English conflict. As soon as the war began in England, these "neutrals" joined the Royalists on the Scottish Privy Council in issuing a strong statement to the effect that Scotland would adhere to a policy of nonintervention.[14]

If Argyll and the kirk were to prevail, they would have to overcome the majority of Scottish aristocrats who preferred neutrality. But in the fall of

1642 the chances of success seemed dim for them. The English Parliament, having previously encouraged the militants, now gave no sign of wanting an alliance with the Scots. As Robert Baillie observed in a letter to Holland: "At that time the king being desperate of our assistance, and the parliament apprehending no need of it, we were no more solicited by either, so we for a long time lay very calm and secure." [15] The history of Scottish politics during the twelve-month period following the outbreak of the Civil War in England, is largely an account of how Scotland was maneuvered into this struggle.[16]

The Argyll faction received aid in their campaign from an unexpected source: Charles I, whose continued ineptitude in dealing with Scotland helped to turn opinion away from neutrality. In December 1642 he had infuriated the Scots by raising no objections when the Earl of Newcastle justified the employment of papist soldiers in his army on the ground that he "believed it very agreeable to present policy." [17] As the Earl of Clarendon realized, incalculable harm was done to the Royalist cause by Newcastle's pronouncement. "From thence these zealous Scots concluded that [Newcastle] preferred the Papists in point of loyalty before the Protestants, which was a calumny of so public a concernment that they could not be silent in." [18]

During March and April 1643 the king rebuffed Scottish efforts at Oxford to help arrange a negotiated peace. In a manner certain to antagonize the peacemakers, Charles rudely treated the delegates from Edinburgh, whom he personally insulted, claiming that they had no business meddling in English affairs. To be sure, Argyll used the harsh treatment received by the Scottish Commissions as evidence of the king's desire to continue the war until he could dictate a treaty.[19]

Also in the spring of 1643, Charles committed a major error that seriously damaged his reputation in the northern kingdom. He had given support to a wild scheme, which entailed having Irish soldiers invade the Highlands, seize the border town of Carlisle, and then lay waste to the south of Scotland. Revealed in early June, the "Antrim Plot" aroused all the worst suspicions about the king's intentions. Robert Baillie characterized the dominant feeling when he observed how "the plot of Antrim had wakened in all a great fear of our safety, and distrust of all the fair words that were or could be given us." [20] A majority in the Scottish Privy Council now shared the kirk's worst fears that no trust could be placed in the king, whose victory in England might very well mark a renewal of his attempts to dominate Scotland.

The Argyll party, capitalizing on the fears raised by the king's recent series of blunders, pushed through a measure in the Privy Council to convoke a Convention of Estates immediately–this despite the fact that one was not scheduled to meet until 1644. The official justification for such an unprecedented step was that matters of great weight faced Scotland, and only the "advice and resolution of the representative body of the kingdom" could deal with them.[21] The weighty matters to be discussed clearly concerned the coming intervention in the English Civil War. With the convocation of the Convention of Estates on June 22, 1643, Argyll's policy seemed to have triumphed. The militants, who had wanted to enter the war for almost a year, saw their goal within reach. A majority of the members of the Estates now favored an interventionist policy. The Duke of Hamilton, recognizing the weakness of his position in the convention, immediately withdrew, leaving his supporters to fend for themselves; and many of them were to be swept along with the tide.[22]

Over a month would transpire before the English Parliament sent a delegation to Edinburgh to request an alliance. It would seem that their delay stemmed from the difficult situation John Pym and his middle party encountered in England during July 1643. Pym, the essential leader of Parliament since 1640, fully realized the necessity of Scottish assistance, but his colleagues had been reluctant to summon a foreign power that demanded a price. In the early days of June 1643 Pym moved the two houses closer toward an alliance by passing the Vow and Covenant and by summoning the Assembly of Divines.[23] But near the end of that same month, he and his party suffered a serious blow.

On June 24 John Hampden, a bulwark of the middle group and Pym's most capable ally in the army, died from wounds received in battle. Largely as a result of Hampden's untimely death, the Earl of Essex, another key member of the middle group, committed a blunder which led to the demand that he be replaced as commander of the army. Pym managed to meet the challenge. Using his considerable political skill he succeeded in restoring his party's position, as well as in strengthening Parliament's military capacity, which had been declining. But it took more than a month's concentrated effort and much political maneuvering to accomplish his purpose.[24] Undoubtedly the main reason for the neglect of Scottish affairs during this time was that Pym had first to put his own house in order before proceeding with new overtures.

The delay in calling for an alliance proved costly, for when Parliament finally decided to seek assistance their military outlook had become critical. The series of Royalist victories culminating in the defeat of Lord Fairfax at Adwalton Moor, and of Sir William Waller at Roundaway Down, demonstrated the weakness of Parliament's army. Moreover, the recent discovery of the Waller Plot, a plan to subvert London, coming at a time when Charles had stated that he wished to negotiate, and of the Antrim Plot, indicating the King's willingness to employ Irish soldiers, served to convince even some of the most pacific M.P.s that Pym had been right.[25] Hence when Parliament came around to seeking Scottish military aid, they were forced to come hat in hand.

The parliamentary commissioners finally arrived in Edinburgh on August 7. Six delegates had been included, four from the Commons and two representing English ministers.[26] In the negotiations that followed, a single delegate overshadowed his colleagues, for as Clarendon acutely observed, "Sir Harry Vane was one of the Commissioners and therefore the others need not be named, since he was all in any business where others were joined with him." [27] To a large extent Clarendon is correct, for the mission to Scotland was Vane's mission.

The true Henry Vane continues to be an elusive creature. Clarendon, always at his best when characterizing contemporaries, described him as a man possessed of "a great understanding which pierced into and discerned the purposes of other men with wonderful sagacity." But few could "make a guess of what he intended," for "he was inferior to no other man in all mysterious artifices." [28] As a politician Vane exhibited great realism and a willingness to compromise when necessary, as well as an ability to conceal his own beliefs. A leader of the war party from the outset of the Civil War, he has sometimes been called a republican; yet he refused to participate in the king's trial when that time arrived. Throughout his life Vane remained a man of strong religious convictions. His early sojourn to New England proved unsatisfactory; his later writings revealing him as a religious individualist, whose main tenet continued to be complete toleration[29]—a belief that on the surface seemed unlikely to win him support from the Covenanters.

The selection of Vane as a commissioner proved to be a wise choice, because as a person he captivated the Scots completely and managed to keep on good terms with them while carrying out these negotiations. Yet Vane's charm should not be overstressed in this context, for he viewed himself as a representative of Parliament. The nature of his assignment had been determined by Parliamentary needs, and he followed his instructions quite faithfully. The primary reason for his mission can be described as military; he had come to Scotland in order to secure the assistance of a Scottish army. But the English realized quite well the connection between Argyll's party and the kirk, and they knew that the latter used its influence to prepare Scottish opinion for the alliance. Without the kirk, in fact, an alliance would be unthinkable. Cognizant of this, Parliament, in its initial statement, accentuated the religious nature of the war going on in England. "The true estate of this quarrel is religion," they wrote, adding that they sought the unification of religion "so the two Kingdoms might be brought into a new conjunction with one form of church government and Directory of Worship."[30]

To emphasize their sincere concern for religion the English brought a declaration from Parliament to the General Assembly of the kirk, calling for "a nearer conjunction betwixt both churches."[31] The Westminster Assembly of Divines sent as their own representatives two prominent ministers, Stephen Marshall and Philip Nye, whose respective reputations had preceded them to Scotland. In fact Nye, as a known and self-confessed Independent, did not receive a warm welcome; his sermon delivered on August 20, to use a contemporary's understatement, "did not please."[32] Marshall, on the other hand, was known and liked as an English Presbyterian.

The inclusion of Philip Nye in a delegation designed to gain the support of a Presbyterian country was probably not as tactless as it may appear. The Scots had learned about the existence of Independents in England from their own ministers who had been in London. And almost every letter sent by the king to Edinburgh carried at least one passage reminding them of the sectarian menace. Indeed, rumors circulated to the effect that the Independents in Parliament opposed the treaty with Scotland on religious grounds.[33] The English never denied the fact that Independents supported Parliament, but they did want to show that sentiment in England unanimously favored the Scottish alliance. Nye's presence provided living proof of this unanimity. It would also demonstrate how religious groups in England put aside their differences for the time being, in order to concentrate on winning the war.

The commissioners' visit concluded with the framing of the Solemn League and Covenant. It is certainly true that the English would have preferred a strictly civil agreement with the Scots; surely they had come for this reason. But Parliament desperately needed military assistance, and was prepared to pay the kirk's high price for it. The driving force working for an alliance, the kirk demanded a religious covenant as a quid pro quo; and the English commissioners recognized that they had no choice but to agree to one. Numerous Parliamentary declarations written to the Convention of Estates and to the General Assembly of the kirk had encouraged the Scots to believe that the English shared their desire for religious uniformity. Clarendon makes the very same point. "Sir Harry Vane," he writes, "was not surprised with the proposition [to establish Presbyterianism] which he had long foreseen, and came resolved to pay their [the Scots'] own price for their friendship." [34]

Clarendon appears to have understood very well what the agreement between the Scots and Parliament entailed. For the Solemn League and Covenant, as drawn up by the Scottish minister Alexander Henderson and approved by the commissioners, came close to committing the English to Presbyterianism. Once having disposed of episcopacy in the second article ("that we shall endeavor in like manner, without respect of persons, the extirpation of Popery [and] prelacy"), the Covenant called for "the nearest conjunction and conformity in religion, Confession of Faith, form of church government, Directory for Worship and catechising." [35] Uniformity of religion had been advocated by the Scots for more than a year, and the English thus recognized this as the minimum they would have to grant.

The kirk wanted very much to obtain assurances from the English commissioners that the Westminster Assembly would establish an ecclesiastical structure identical with the Scottish model. A Presbyterian church government in England, with a clergy independent of civil authority, would not only be the ideal type, it would also permit the Scottish hierarchy to exert influence in English affairs. Sir Henry Vane, Jr., could not make such a definite pledge. He was, however, willing to go quite far in meeting the demands of the Scottish church. In the version of the Covenant which the English commissioners approved appeared the statement that "the Church of Scotland in doctrine, worship, discipline and government [was] according to the word of God." [36] In other words, Vane and his colleagues accepted the Scottish view that their church approximated divine will. But Vane insisted upon the inclusion of *two* clauses in the section that dealt specifically with the future settlement in England. The reformation of religion would be "according to the word of God, and the example of the best reformed churches." [37] The additional clauses, in this context, made the meaning somewhat ambiguous, thereby leaving final decisions to English ministers and the English Parliament.

Anyone familiar with events in England should have realized that a church government similar to Scottish Presbyterianism was unlikely to be adopted. One of Parliament's main objections to the Laudian church had been that the clergy remained free of Parliamentary authority, and they could not be expected to remove one independent clergy in order to set up another. Therefore, any responsible representative of this body would have behaved very much as Vane did under the circumstances, and would have rejected any treaty that promised to establish a Scottish-style Presbyterianism in England.[38] It did not take much political insight to know that Parliament would never have accepted Henderson's unambiguous statement. Vane was being honest and realistic with the Covenanters, rather than confusing the issue. It is indicative of how little the Scots understood the English situation that they interpreted Vane's insertion of the two clauses as "keeping of a door open in England to independency." [39] This may have been part of his intention, but he would have been dishonest if he had promised a Presbyterian settlement which he knew his country would never support.

As it turned out, Vane granted more to the Scots than his fellow countrymen would later accept. When the Covenant, which he approved, arrived in London it encountered a sizable amount of opposition. The Westminster Assembly objected to the assertion made in the Covenant that the Church of Scotland was "according to the word of God." A few of the English ministers, most notably Dr. Cornelius Burgess, protested vigorously, and called for the elimination of the clause. The divines devised a compromise solution whereby a qualifying statement would be added to the controversial phrase, explaining that the Scottish church followed God's word "as far as in my conscience I shall conceive it to be according to the word of God." [40]

In the House of Commons the original Covenant drew a similar adverse reaction. Sir Simonds Dewes expressed a widely held sentiment when he wrote in his diary: "I conceived this to be a very strange clause, that we should declare that the Church of Scotland was reformed according to the word of God." [41] On September 1, 1643, when the lower house voted on this issue, a large majority decided that the Westminster Assembly had been too restrained. They eliminated the entire phrase "according to the word of God" as it applied to the kirk, so that the final version of the Covenant said nothing whatever about the divine origin of the Scottish church.[42]

The Solemn League and Covenant represented only one aspect of the treaty arranged between the two countries. On August 26 the convention voted to approve the military terms presented by the English delegates and modified by a special Scottish committee appointed for this purpose. A list of eleven items had been worked out enumerating the conditions of Scottish entry into the war, although the exact size of the Covenanting army would be specified at a later date. The treaty included details as to payment as well as official statements regarding various guarantees, such as the promise not to conclude peace without mutual advice and consent.[43] Nevertheless, this agreement was only provisional. The English commissioners would refer these tentatively accepted articles back to the two houses at Westminster "to be respectively taken into their consideration and proceeded with as they shall find cause." [44]

With the exception of Philip Nye, who returned to London to make a rousing speech in favor of the Covenant,[45] all of the original commissioners remained in Scotland for the purpose of working over the details of the alliance. They did not leave Edinburgh for another two months. And as soon as they had made their reports to Parliament on October 26, a second commission, consisting of eleven members including Vane (in name only), was sent back to Scotland to complete arrangements.[46]

The length of time the commissioners spent in Scotland is evidence of the difficulties involved in ironing out differences. For much of the give-and-take connected with the civil terms of the treaty showed that numerous problems existed between the two countries which were as hard to resolve as the religious one. Despite temporary solutions, many of the subjects treated during these months persisted as sources of irritation throughout the Civil War.[47]

One of the most difficult matters on which to reach accord was the fortification of Berwick. This strategically located town on the Scottish border had been demilitarized as a result of the Large Treaty of 1641. But the outbreak of the Civil War caused the Scots to realize how vulnerable they would be if an unfriendly army occupied Berwick, and in the spring of 1643 they had seriously considered taking it over themselves. By August some Parliamentary troops gained control of the town, and Parliament imagined that this action would now make the Scots feel secure. Instead, the latter showed little appreciation, behaving as if the troops had been Papists belonging to the Earl of Newcastle. They demanded that Berwick be turned over to the army in which they had the most faith, namely, their own. "After a long and serious debate," the English commissioners gave way. Shortly thereafter Scottish troops entered Berwick and took charge of the town, to hold it until the end of the first Civil War.[48] The Venetian ambassador was duly impressed by the great trust Parliament had shown in turning over a garrison that "opens the way into England at their pleasure."[49] Presumably, this trust went only in one direction.

Another matter having serious implications for the rest of the Civil War concerned the extent of Scottish influence in devising peace treaties. The peace party in England opposed introducing Scotland into dealings with the king, since an agreement which had to make allowances for special Scottish needs would be that much more difficult to arrange. And if the Scots insisted, as might be expected, that Charles accept Presbyterianism, there could be scant hope of an early end to the war. Consequently, when the commissioners first went to Scotland in August, the peace party saw to it that their instructions contained no specific promise of mutual consultations.[50] But for understandable reasons the Scots wanted to obtain greater assurance against a strictly English peace. They did not wish to be caught unawares by a sudden rapprochement between their allies and their enemy, and they demanded the right to participate in all future negotiations. The final terms of the treaty, as ratified by Parliament, therefore represented a victory for them: "That no cessation, nor any pacification, or agreement for peace whatsoever, shall be made by either Kingdom, or the armies of either Kingdom, without the mutual advice and consent of each Kingdom."[51]

While this hard bargaining between the two allies was taking place, the startling news came through of a cessation of arms in Ireland. The announcement, arriving at a time when Scottish preparations for war had got under way, served to strengthen their resolve, for it confirmed their suspicions that the king collaborated with Papists. Yet the prospect of a cease-fire raised the whole problem of the Scottish army in northern Ireland.[52] These troops, in desperate straits, lacking food, clothing, and equipment, would now be exposed to the full force of the Irish. Unless drastic measures were taken, the Scots would be forced to withdraw. Neither they nor the English particularly relished this prospect. The latter feared, quite rightly, that unless the Irish were kept busy in Ireland, they would soon keep themselves busy in England. The Scots, for their part, did not wish to give up their important interests in Ulster. Parliament responded to the call for assistance by granting the Scots a lump sum of money, part of which would pay the arrears. The Scots originally asked for £100,000, but after a bit of wrangling the amount was reduced by one-third, to the sum of 66,666 pounds, 13 shillings, and 7 pence. Ten thousand suits of clothes and shoes, and an equal number of bowls of meal, were sent to help make up the difference.[53]

One aspect of the Irish situation created controversy between England and Scotland. At an early stage of the discussion the Scots asked that both the Parliamentary and Scottish forces in Ireland be placed under the command of a Scottish general. Military control would be a sure way of extending, or at least maintaining, their influence in Ireland. There were, however, persons in England, even in Parliament, whose own interests conflicted with Scottish expansionist desires, and the measure ran into a good deal of opposition. Sir John Clotworthy, himself a holder of considerable land in Ulster, opposed the proposal vehemently.[54] But Sir Henry Vane, Jr., had agreed to the Scots' request while in Edinburgh, and he succeeded in carrying it through the House of Commons. From December 1643 until 1646 the two armies remained under the control of Colonel Monro, a Scotsman.[55]

The treaty between Scotland and the English Parliament, completed in Edinburgh during November 1643, was finally ratified in England on the 29th.[56] Parliament had conceded a great deal, but the price did not seem exorbitant; for the Scots would soon be sending 21,000 soldiers into England to help turn the tide in their favor.

The kirk party for their part thus had good reason to be satisfied; they had been induced, by money and favorable terms, to participate in a war that they were already anxious to enter. In the declaration sent by the Convention of Estates to the English Parliament, they explained their decision to intervene in a foreign war in the most altruistic manner. Scotland would send her troops because she had become "deeply affected with the sense of the sad calamitous conditions of [her] brethren of England."[57] As part of the agreement between the two kingdoms, and as an example of the mutual desire for a closer union between churches, the Scots received an invitation to send representatives to participate in the great work of the Westminster Assembly. When the delegates to the Assembly arrived in London they appeared optimistic and confident, for they were sure that God would reward their efforts. The reality of Civil War England would alter these great hopes.

NOTES

1. *Constitutional Documents,* p. 124.
2. For an excellent new account of these events as well as a thorough presentation of background material, see David Stevenson, *The Scottish Revolution, 1637-44* (Newton Abbot, 1973).
3. William J. Mathieson, *Politics and Religion,* 2 vols. (Glasgow, 1902), vol. II, pp. 16-17, 39.
4. S. R. Gardiner, *History of England from the Accession of James I,* 10 vols. (London, 1896), vol. IX, p. 54.
5. Sir James Balfour, *The Historical Works,* 4 Vols. (London, 1825), vol. II, pp. 377-378.
6. Mark Napier, *Memoirs of the Marquis of Montrose,* 2 vols. (Edinburgh, 1856), vol. I, pp. 269-270. Especially the Marquis of Argyll.
7. See, for example, Samuel Rutherford, *Lex Rex,* October 1644.
8. Gilbert Burnet, *History of His Own Time,* 2 vols. (London, 1724), I, pp. 43-44.
9. Gilbert Burnet, *The Memoirs of James and William, Dukes of Hamilton* (London, 1677), pp. 234-236.
10. Baillie, I, p. 115.
11. D.N.B.
12. Nobles in alliance with Hamilton were the Earls of Buchan, Dunfermline, Galloway, Home, Lindsay, and Roxburgh.
13. Burnet, *Hamilton,* pp. 195-196.
14. *Register of the Privy Council of Scotland,* 1642, II, pp. 264-265.
15. Baillie, II, p. 57.
16. For a more detailed account of this year, see Lawrence Kaplan, "Steps to War: The Scots and Parliament, 1643-1644," *Journal of British Studies,* IX (1970), pp. 50-70.
17. John Rushworth, *Historical Collections,* 7 vols., 1649-1701, V, pp. 78-83.

18. Clarendon, II, p. 505.
19. Baillie, II, p. 66.
20. Ibid., p. 80.
21. *Register of the Privy Council of Scotland,* 1643, II, pp. 426-427.
22. Baillie, II, p. 75.
23. L.J., VI, pp. 86-87; *Acts and Ordinances,* I, pp. 180-184.
24. J. H. Hexter, *The Reign of King Pym* (Cambridge, Mass., 1941), chap. VI, *passim.*
25. *Civil War,* I, p. 178.
26. The other three were Sir William Armine, Thomas Hatcher, and Henry Darley; the two ministers were Stephen Marshall and Philip Nye. The assigned delegates from the Lords declined to go.
27. Clarendon, III, p. 216, fn.
28. Ibid., pp. 216-217.
29. Violet A. Rowe, *Sir Henry Vane, the Younger* (London, 1970), *passim.*
30. *Parliament of Scotland, Acts and Statutes,* VI, pp. 36-37.
31. L.J., VI, p. 140.
32. Baillie, II, p. 97.
33. *Mercurius Britanicus,* September 26, 1643; *The Complete Intelligencer,* November 14, 1643.
34. Clarendon, III, p. 221.
35. *Constitutional Documents,* pp. 267-271. This is the final English version.
36. *Parliament of Scotland,* VI, p. 42. I owe this reference to Mr. Walter Makey.
37. Burnet, *Hamilton,* pp. 239-240.
38. Sir Simonds Dewes, whose political and religious views were opposed to those of Vane, strongly favored the insertion of the two clauses; 165, fols. 162-162 v.
39. Baillie, II, p. 90.
40. C.J., VI, p. 223; Yonge, 18,778, fol. 44.
41. Dewes, 165, fol. 158v-159.
42. By the time the Scots arrived in London there was little that they could do to change Parliament's additions. Making a virtue out of a necessity, Baillie, after seeing the alterations in the Covenant, claimed that they were "for the better" (Baillie, II, pp. 101-102).

43. *Parliament of Scotland,* IV, pp. 47-48.
44. *Ibid.,* p. 48.
45. September 25, 1643, T.T., E. 70 (22).
46. L.J., VI, p. 228. Vane does not seem to have made a second trip. His name does not appear in subsequent dispatches coming from Edinburgh.
47. Dr. Stevenson, in his account, emphasizes the rapidity of the agreement, but in doing so, gives the impression that the English Parliament ratified the entire treaty immediately, *Op. cit.,* pp. 287-289.
48. H.M.C., Portland MSS, I, pp. 129, 136-137.
49. C.S.P. Ven., p. 28.
50. Dewes, 165, fol. 126; C.J., III, pp. 141-142.
51. L.J., VI, p. 290. See the earlier Scottish version, *Parliament of Scotland,* IV, p. 48.
52. Baillie, II, pp. 102-103.
53. *Parliament of Scotland,* VI, pp. 247-249; L.J., VI, p. 244; C.J., III, p. 350.
54. Wodrow MSS, LXV, fol. 85.
55. C.J., III, p. 350.
56. Rushworth, II, p. 485.
57. *Parliament of Scotland,* VI, p. 50. So deeply affected were the Scots that they all but ignored a last ditch attempt by France to restrain them (L.J., VI, p. 323).

I

The Scots and the War Party

The Covenanters had entered the Civil War in the summer of 1643, allied to Parliament, because they realized that sooner or later, willingly or not, they would be drawn in. It was far the wiser course of action to choose for themselves the time and conditions of entry. With the favorable outcome, which few Scots doubted, Scotland would be secure from threats of invasion and Scotsmen would reap God's glory for having been his instrument in establishing Presbyterianism in England. Scottish ministers hoped to convert their southern brethren to a Presbyterian church government and had received a vague commitment to this effect in the Solemn League and Covenant.[1] The Covenanters had every reason to expect success, for they held the balance of power and Parliament obviously needed their assistance to win the war. The Venetian ambassador testified to this need in letter after letter. On the 13th of October, 1643, he wrote, "Amid all these difficulties their [Parliament's] chief hopes are based on the Scots." On the 24th of the same month: "The principal foundation on which the English build is assistance from the Scots"; and a fortnight later he added,

"Every day they artfully announce the entry of the Scots, having no other means to compensate their own weakness, which they cannot hide much as they would like to." [2]

Those who helped bring Scotland into the war believed they had acquired a valuable ally, for the Scottish army had a European reputation, and Scots soldiers were sought after by several countries. Alexander Leslie, the Earl of Leven, who commanded their army, had performed effectively with the Swedish forces during the Thirty Years War. But he was far from unique, for practically every senior officer from major to general had seen action on the continent.[3] These proven troops had already established their reputation in the easy defeats they inflicted on the English in 1639 and 1640. Little wonder that the Scottish army was expected to turn the tide in a war which recently had been going against Parliament. But to achieve their religious and secular goals the Covenanters had to become fully immersed in English Parliamentary affairs, because it was here, away from the battlefield, that victory would actually be won.

The engagement between Scotland and England had been joined at a time when the political scene in London had become unsettled. The alliance itself represented the last great monument of John Pym's statesmanship. He had been the unchallenged leader of the Long Parliament, but from the latter part of September, when the Covenant was sworn, Pym's personal imprint seemed to be missing in politics; and on December 8, 1643, he died. His illness and death struck a great blow to the unity of Parliament. The ever watchful Venetian ambassador predicted the worst.

> John Pym is dead, a solicitor of civil causes, but the promotor of the present rebellion and the director of the whole machine. . . . The hydra is not therefore left without a head, but so far no one has appeared of equal application and ability. Indeed, it would seem that rivalry for the lead gives hope of divisions and parties, which affords the easiest and safest means for restoring the King to his former greatness.[4]

How accurate the ambassador proved to be in his prediction will be explored in this and the following chapters. But before we can delve into the various shapes and forms which characterized Parliamentary politics after Pym's death, and the place of the Scots therein, it will first be necessary to describe briefly the situation existing while he lived.[5]

The major political issue in the Civil War Parliament involved questions of peace and war, and parties tended to split in regard to their predilection for one or the other of these two ends. There was one party so anxious for an immediate settlement that they were quite willing to grant the king any number of concessions. Persons of this complexion fell just short of being *bona fide* Royalists, although the party found itself continually faced with the depletion of its ranks by desertions to Oxford, as in the summer of 1643. Those who remained behind in London tried their best to terminate the war and to bring about a peace: one that would preserve some of the minimal gains of the Long Parliament, such as the prevention of arbitrary taxation, the abolition of prerogative courts, and guaranteed regular Parliaments, while at the same time extending Parliamentary control over the church establishment. Denzil Holles, the leader of the party, had been considered an irreconcilable incendiary in the early days of the Long Parliament; but the advent of a bloody Civil War, and the inevitable hardening of positions caused him to assume a moderate stance. Along with Holles, the most active members of this faction were John Maynard and Sir William Lewis, and we repeatedly find them named as supporters of motions for facilitating peace treaties and as tellers opposing the various measures for strengthening Parliament's military position.

At the other end of the spectrum could be found a faction who, from all appearances, did not desire peace until the king should be soundly beaten on the battlefield. The only treaty that this war party might conceivably back was one whose severe terms could not possibly gain the king's acceptance. Consequently, they did their utmost to sabotage all attempts at serious negotiation, while every measure which improved Parliament's chances of victory, met their vigorous approval. War-party adherents varied from one or two republicans like Henry Marten, who wanted to strip the king of his prerogative, giving Parliament complete sovereignty; to those who, while favoring a monarchy, desired institutional safeguards (e.g., Parliamentary control over the army) to permanently hamstring the king. Their leaders in 1643 were militants like Sir Arthur Haselrig, William Strode, and Sir Henry Vane, Jr.[6]

With two such extreme groups sitting at Westminster, it seems astonishing that Parliament managed to conduct a sustained war effort. The fact that they did carry on reasonably effectively can be credited to the outstanding leadership ability of John Pym. For it was Pym who preserved Parliamentary unity through the stresses and strains of the first year and one-half of the Civil War. In itself a major achievement, it involved artistry in politics which later proved to be irreplaceable. What enabled Pym to shape policy and maintain unity was his control of the middle party, the third political grouping in the Long Parliament. Numerically this faction tended to be small, consisting, at most, of only about one-fifth of the House of Commons, and probably less.[7] But since the other two parties remained fairly evenly balanced, the middle group could decide all-important questions merely by placing its weight on either side of the scale. The behavior of this group did not appear to be as consistent as that of the other two parties, for Pym and his followers pursued a dual approach to questions of war and peace. On the one hand, Pym's strenuous legislative efforts served to encourage a vigorous prosecution of the war, and this caused moderates like Sir Simonds Dewes to consider Pym a "violent spirit." But unlike the militants, Pym himself maintained a "benevolent neutrality" toward efforts for peace; while other middle-group members might be quite energetic in their support of treaties.[8]

If the Scots were to influence the conduct of the war and subsequent peace, they would have to join forces with the English party that shared their views. But to do so would not be easy, considering their inexperience in English affairs. The policies that they wished to pursue precluded the peace party almost at once. The Scots had come into the Civil War because they did not trust the king, and feared that once the Royalists defeated Parliament, Scotland would be next. On this point alone they would oppose the peace group,since the latter based their whole program on a faith in the king's integrity which defied the ample evidence to the contrary. The Scots also supported the war to the tune of 21,000 troops soon to be in combat against the Royalist enemy, and they naturally expected Parliament to continue its end of the fighting. Finally, their commissioners realized soon after arriving in London that the peace party opposed Scotland's entry into the war, and continued to vote against measures which they wished to see enacted. In October, from London, the Scottish minister Alexander Henderson spoke of "a secret malignant party" (meaning the peace party) which "do so retard the business, that it is to be feared the money come not in such proportion nor so timeously as is there expected."[9]

Obviously the Covenanters would have little to do with the moderates. While they rejected peace at any price, an important consideration for the Scots concerned the manner in which the war was to be terminated. Before intervening in England, Scottish leaders had wished to arrange various compromise solutions, and there had existed from 1642 onward a firm desire on their part to mediate the differences between the king and Parliament. But Charles had rebuffed all their efforts, thereby contributing to the arguments of those in Edinburgh seeking an alliance with Parliament.[10] Nevertheless, it remained in Scotland's interest to see that neither side gained an overwhelming victory and they continued to press for a negotiated settlement.

One of the first instructions sent from Edinburgh to the Scottish commissioners in London called for a treaty. "It is our earnest desire," it read, "that by the joint advice of both Kingdoms, all good means may be used for performing such a happy pacification betwixt his Majesty and this people as may serve most for the glory of God."[11] This note arrived in January 1644; another set of directions issued later that same month had the title, "Instructions sent to the Scots Commissioners at London about the grounds of a just peace and affixing a day for his Majesty's return to his Parliament."[12] In April 1644 the Scottish government seemed so zealous for peace that they were cautioned by their own commissioners not to place excessive hopes on negotiations which had little chance of succeeding.[13] Thus, the Covenanters, when they entered the war, essentially pursued a middle-party policy; i.e., favoring a treaty while at the same time preparing for war.

Since the Scottish position in 1643 tended to be similar to that of the English middle party, one would expect to find the Scots joined with the middle group in politics. But this natural union did not take place, for the simple reason that a middle party as such started to disappear from the English political scene at about the same time as the Scottish commissioners began arriving from Edinburgh.

A middle group had come into existence during an early stage of the Civil War when a compromise peace still seemed possible. Those who believed that negotiations from a position of strength, without necessarily crushing the king's forces, was the best approach, gravitated toward this stance. But the failure of the Oxford treaty, in the spring of 1643, plus the king's apparent design to use Papists, led to a realization that the war would continue much longer than first anticipated, and would therefore require more vigorous actions. This awareness, in turn, resulted in a greater political polarization.

The middle party had been effective mainly because of Pym's commanding stature as leader of the Long Parliament. Without him, his followers had two alternative courses of action to pursue: they could either join one of the two existing parties or remain uncommitted. Those who chose the latter continued to act more or less in the same manner as before; that is to say, they voted for legislation which strengthened Parliament militarily, while at the same time favoring attempts to reach a peaceful solution with the king. These were to be the unaffiliated men in the center whose votes often determined close divisions, but who no longer gave direction to Parliament as they had while Pym lived. After December 1643 the names which appear in the diaries most frequently are those of MPs associated with extreme factions: Vane, St. John, Haselrig, Holles, Stapleton, and Lewis. These were Pym's successors, but the changing circumstances forced them to differ from him in their total commitment to one policy or the other, and this militated against the unity which Pym had so desperately tried to maintain.[14] Eight months after his death the Scots bemoaned the failure of anyone to replace him. "Since Pym died," wrote the shrewd Scots minister Robert Baillie, "not a state head amongst them: many very good and able spirits but not any so great or comprehensive a brain, as to manage the multitude of so weighty affairs as lies on them." [15]

Ironically the Scottish alliance, which Pym had brought into being, served to weaken the tenability of a middle position by creating the necessity for total victory in the war. For any inclination of the Scots toward a middle way mattered less than the fact that their presence at the conference table made such a course more difficult to achieve. Purely Scottish interests would have to be thrashed out and settled, in addition to a proposed change in English church government, which Charles might never accept. With the Covenanters in the war a negotiated peace, as envisaged by moderates, became a very remote prospect indeed; and this could delight only the militants. Scottish intervention, therefore, has to be viewed as a decisive event in the history of the Civil War. It was a long time coming, but once it had materialized the outcome of the war could never be the same.

For the Scots, the choice of an alliance with the war party was in reality no choice at all. It had been made for them even before they entered the war by those who anticipated the influence they would carry in English affairs. Thus, when Sir Henry Vane, Jr., the war-party leader, went to Edinburgh to negotiate the treaty, he did so with every intention of ingratiating himself and his party with the Scots. One of the cleverest politicians in Parliament,[16] Sir Henry gave the Covenanters actual proof of how he and his associates were to be their benefactors by granting them almost enything they desired. He left the Scots with the definite impression that if they relied on the war party their interests would be well looked after. But Vane went one step further: he also ensured that his Scottish friends would enter the war with a prejudice against the peace party. Denzil Holles, whose later association with the Covenanters must have provided him with a fairly accurate account of Vane's mission, wrote in reference to the war party:

> Those creatures of theirs, whom they sent Commissioners into Scotland for that business, represented the state of affairs to that Parliament as being directly contrary to what it was, endearing their own party to them as the only sincere, public-spirited men, who desired such a reformation as was agreeable to their government, and such a peace as might be a joint safety and security to both Kingdoms; giving characters of all others as malignants, ill affected, averse to the Scottish nation, opposers of a good understanding between the Kingdom, and of their mutual assistance of each other.[17]

The description of English politics which the Scots had gathered from Vane was confirmed when their first commissioners arrived in London in September. Practically everything they had been told seemed to be borne out by the actual situation. The peace party did seem averse to Scottish intervention, and continued to oppose their interests; as, for example, in regard to the granting of supplies to their army.[18] The war party, on the other hand, proved from the start to be a faithful ally. For although Sir Henry Vane, Jr., remained in Edinburgh until mid-October putting the finishing touches on the treaty of alliance, he made sure that the Scots would be well looked after by his party. In London, waiting with open arms for the Scottish commissioners, was Vane's new colleague Oliver St. John, the king's solicitor general.

From the outset of the Long Parliament St. John had been one of its most important leaders. He had gained national prominence in 1637 when, as a lawyer, he defended Lord Say and John Hampden in the Ship Money case. In January 1641 the king had made him solicitor general with the intention of blunting his animosity to the Crown. But the cooption did not succeed; St. John remained one of Parliament's most active members, working in close association with Pym.[19] Throughout his life St. John played the role of a common-law advocate, and his approach to law tended to permeate his whole personality. He gave the impression of a cold and reserved person with a logical mind, whose speeches were well argued but lacking in forcefulness and imagery to be found in those of his contemporaries, such as Vane. To Clarendon, St. John was "of a dark and clouded countenance, very proud and conversing with very few," a man "seldom known to smile." [20] His religious beliefs are difficult to determine precisely. In two separate letters, written at different times to his relative, Oliver Cromwell, St. John gave every indication of being a devout Puritan; while his support of toleration in September 1644 and later serves to classify him as an Independent. He was certainly neither an Anglican nor a sectarian. In a letter written in 1650 he spoke of England's great deliverance from "Papists and atheists on the one hand, and from sectaries on the other." Most likely Dr. Pearl is correct when she describes him as being in favor of "an Erastian nonepiscopal church with some measure of toleration." [21]

St. John became one of the first members of the middle party to ally himself with the war forces. According to Robert Baillie he was "Pym's successor," and as such he maintained cordial relations with his former colleagues, employing his contacts to gain moderate support for militant policies. In the late summer of 1643, influenced perhaps by Pym's illness, he began his association with Vane, and by the time of Pym's death their partnership was accepted as one of the facts of political life.[22] In the autumn of 1643 the war party appears to have agreed that every possible step must be taken to encourage the Scots. Thus, while Vane tarried in Edinburgh flattering them, the leaders of the war party in London were actively advancing Scotland's cause. And with Vane away, St. John became the spokesman for Scottish interests. On October 6 in Guild Hall he called upon the City to contribute funds for Parlaiment's loyal Scottish allies.[23] A week later he brought in an ordinance to the House of Commons for securing money to pay the Scottish army. And on the 26th of October, the same day Vane returned from Scotland, St. John once more pressed the Commons to raise money for their northern brethren.[24] Vane gave himself only one day's rest, and on the 27th his turn came to speak to the city. He used these words in praise of the Scots:

> Yet so sensible they were, of the danger of religion here, of the near relation that they had to their brethren of England, and of that common calamity threatened to overcome both Kingdoms, that they were ready to break through all difficulties, and to expose themselves to all dangers.[25]

In the months that followed, the militants kept up their efforts on behalf of their allies. In November, when the possibility arose that a portion of the funds earmarked for Scotland might be turned over to other English armies, Vane and St. John again leaped to the Scots' defense. On this occasion they had the support of Walter Long (who had previously been with the middle party) and William Strode.[26] The Covenanters, seeing their needs thus looked after, had every reason to believe that they had made a wise move in allying themselves with the war party.

Making possible the alliance between Scottish Covenanters and the English militants was the existence of a religious truce, arranged by the Presbyterian and Independent ministers in London, which had been in operation since 1641. Responsible Puritan divines recognized that unless

Parliament defeated the king all hope of achieving religious reforms would have to be abandoned. Since religious controversy might undermine parliamentary unity during this time of crisis, they entered into an engagement to discontinue sermons and tracts which stressed differences for the duration of the conflict.[27] Also serving to diffuse the ecclesiastical issue was the creation in June 1643 of a special body, the Westminster Assembly of Divines, to work out the nature of the new church government. By establishing this separate institution, Parliament ensured, at least for the time being, that heated religious discussions would be held outside its halls, and would therefore not arise to complicate the political scene.

When they first entered the Civil War, the Scottish divines agreed to accept both the religious truce as well as the ground rules for religious reform.[28] This enabled the non-Presbyterian war party leaders to associate with the Scottish commissioners without revealing their own religious predilections. Although the Scots later claimed that they had been used,[29] initially the alliance proved to be mutually beneficial. For their part, the main advantage gained by the militants was obtaining control over the direction of military affairs.

Nominally Parliament possessed supreme power in matters relating to tactics and to the deployment of forces, but in practice the Lord General held a large measure of autonomy. It had long been one of the chief objects of the war party to replace Essex as general, or failing that, to circumvent his authority. Robert Devereux, the Earl of Essex, had been Lord General of Parliament's forces since July, 1642, and almost from the beginning he had not been popular with the war party. This stemmed partly from his original demand that he should have power to negotiate terms of peace with the king, which made them suspect his commitment.[30] But his popularity with the "fiery spirits" declined even further when it became obvious that Essex possessed limited military ability. Few were willing to make allowances for his handicaps, such as inadequate provisions and the lack of a genuinely permanent army. Instead, his failure to defeat the king was attributed to his imagined disloyalty, and several members of Parliament seriously believed that Essex did not wish to win the war. As the minister Richard Baxter observed, "It was discovered that the Earl of Essex's judgment (and the wisest men's about him) was never for the ending of the war by the sword, but only to force a pacificatory treaty."[31]

During the summer of 1643 the war party launced a campaign to create a separate army which would perform the tasks that Essex seemed unwilling to do. They brought forth Sir William Waller as their champion, and Henry Marten acted as his principal supporter in Parliament. In July Marten, with the backing of some of the militants in London, was well on the way to providing Waller with a sizable army, independent of the Lord General. The troops for Waller's army would be drawn from the City, which had also been the main source of supply for Essex. If Marten were allowed to proceed, not only would Essex lose his commanding position over all the Parliamentary armies, he would also be left without an adequate force of his own. The plans for Waller were on the verge of succeeding, when they encountered the rather stolid figure of John Pym in their path. Before Marten could regain his momentum, he discovered Essex supplied with 4,000 fresh soldiers, a month's pay for his troops, and orders to relieve the west (which had been intended for Waller). In addition, Waller had been made subordinate to the Lord General. A few days afterward Marten, as a result of some antimonarchical remarks, found himself in the Tower, with plenty of time to think about his own shortcomings as a leader of Parliament.[32]

Pym had backed the Lord General on a number of occasions, and Essex was content to follow Pym's lead in politics. Once Pym left the political scene, however, Essex moved rapidly into alliance with the peace party in Parliament. His conjunction with the peace group coincided with, and contributed to, the similar movement of other middle-party members in the same direction. The first indication we have of this new coalition of forces in Parliament appears in the course of the debate concerning the Earl of Holland in November 1643.

During the previous summer, the Earl of Holland had tried unsuccessfully to convince his good friend Essex to support a program of peace that bordered on treason. Essex, demonstrating once again his loyalty to Parliament, rejected Holland's scheme; and compromised as he was, the latter had made off to join the king at Oxford. But after a brief sojourn with the Royalists, who studiously ignored him, Holland reversed his course once again and came back to London. In November 1643 the Lord General encouraged him to return to Parliament. Thus, without any ceremony or apologies, just as if nothing had happened in the intervening months, the Earl of Holland resumed his place in the House of Lords. His fellow peers accepted him back warmly.[33] However, such was not the case in the Commons, where the war party did not care to be charitable to a lord who had long been an opponent of theirs, and whom they now regarded as a traitor. They demanded that Holland be impeached for committing high treason. Mr. John Gurdon, one of the most consistently warlike members of Parliament, announced that he would "rather pardon all the Lords at Oxford than this one." [34]

A division then took place in the Commons on the question whether the Earl of Holland should be committed to the Tower. At first, the voting appeared to follow the usual pattern, with war-party men like Strode, Haselrig, Wentworth, and Gurdon supporting the proposal, while Holles, Maynard, and Rudyard opposed it. But a split occurred among M.P.s who previously had been with the middle party: St. John voted with the war party, and Sir Philip Stapleton joined Holles to act as teller against the proposal.[35]

Stapleton, a prominent associate of Pym in the middle group, frequently acted as spokesman for the Lord General in the House of Commons. On this issue he again represented Essex's wishes, since anything but an acquittal would have been a slur on the general's honor. But this particular vote is significant in that it marks the first time Stapleton's name is joined with that of Denzil Holles, and this episode began a relationship which lasted until both were expelled from Parliament in August 1647. For the next four years Stapleton served as one of the leaders of the peace party. His new affiliation revealed the fact that this group had become the party of the Lord General.[36]

Until the fall of 1643 the moderates, more concerned with achieving peace than fighting a war, had not found it necessary to support Essex. But by this point in the Civil War, the failure of negotiations and the entry of the Scots made it evident that the conflict would be a prolonged one. As a consequence, the leadership of the peace party decided to work with the general whose political views most nearly resembled their own. The weakening of middle-group cohesion at this time presented them with the opportunity.[37]

As the peace issue was forgotten for the moment, the conduct of the war became a more crucial concern. According to the diarist Sir Simonds Dewes, the question of military leadership and support for various armies divided Parliament more than any other issue. He saw three separate parties, each clustering around a different army. The first faction

> was those that desired all that might possibly be spared for the satisfying of the Scots, and were therefore wroth the Lord General's army should either be too numerous or require too much money, and their leader of this party was young Sir Henry Vane . . . . the second consisted of such as desired to further Sr. William Waller's expedition into the west for the reducing of those parts and of such as desired to maintain the powerful associations which were already settled in diverse committess by ordinances of Parliament, and of this party the chief leaders were Mr. Trenchard and Mr. Prideaux, being western men. The third party consisted of Philip Stapleton and others that had commanded in the Lord General's army and of all those who were not comprehended in the associations.[38]

Much of Dewes's analysis coincides with observations already made in this chapter. We have just seen how Vane and his associates worked with the Scots, and how the "fiery spirits" put forth Sir William Waller's cause in the summer of 1643, and finally how Stapleton and the peace party supported Essex. There is one discrepancy, however. From Dewes's account it would appear that the first two groups went along separate ways; our evidence indicates otherwise.[39]

For while different members of the war party served as chief advocates of either the Scottish army or Waller's, they also cooperated with each other time and again. Thus those who can be identified as spokesmen for one of the two armies can be shown to have worked together on a whole range of issues as well. Vane and St. John, as we saw, always spoke for the Scots; they were often joined by William Strode and others. The M.P.s who most often looked out for the interests of Waller's army were Sir Arthur Haselrig, John Trenchard, Edmund Prideaux, and Sir Peter Wentworth.[40] All of these men belonged to the war party, and they all actively supported all sorts of warlike measures. Sir Arthur Haselrig, for example, served as a teller for the "violent spirits" seven times out of a possible eleven divisions in the half-year period from November 11, 1643 (the Earl of Holland debate) until April 13, 1644. On six of these occasions he was joined by either Vane or St. John, and on the seventh he had Wentworth with him. In the other divisions during these six months the tellers for the war party were either Strode, Prideaux, Vane, St. John, or Wentworth.[41]

Another pattern which reveals the absence of any fissure dividing the proponents of the Scots and those of Waller was the cordial relationship existing between Sir William and the Scottish commissioners, in spite of the fact that their two armies had to compete for the same supplies from Parliament. In a letter enumerating the people in London who gave aid and comfort to the Scots, Baillie concluded his list with the statement, "None is so panting for us as brave Waller." In fact, Baillie gave the impression that for Parliament the chief hope for victory came from Waller's army. "But the main chance," he wrote, "is about good and valiant Sir William Waller. The grandees would see, they say, that poor man perish." [42] However, the esteem in which the Scots held Waller did not extend to Essex. Again from Baillie:

> A strong party in the Parliament and City whichever would have been at peace in any terms, did make great use of this dejection (the loss of Arundel Castle) pressing to have the General's army made strong; but Waller's and Manchester's and all others so weak as they might, that if they could not persuade, yet by the power of the General's army, when it had all the strength conveyed to it, they might command a peace to be taken in what terms they find it most convenient for their own particular.[43]

These letters are revealing, and for several reasons. They show, of course, that the Scots supported Waller and distrusted Essex and the peace party. But they illustrate something even more interesting: namely, to what extent Scottish attitudes and opinions were shaped for them by their political allies. This is not surprising, considering that the Scots were new to English affairs and would need some time to get the feel of things for themselves. In any case, on every important political issue they held the same view as their English friends. We have seen how the Scots believed that Essex could not be trusted because he inclined toward peace. This was more or less what the war party had maintained for almost a year. The Scots also had learned to be wary of the peace party, so much so that their suspicions exceeded the bounds of normal Parliamentary disagreement. In December Alexander Henderson spoke openly of "a secret malignant party" which continued to begrudge the Scottish army supplies, i.e., the peace party. A few months later the Scots still referred to the peace party as "the Oxfordian faction" and "the evil party." [44]

The month of January 1644 provides us with an excellent example of how assiduously the leaders of the war party worked to guide Scottish attitudes. At this juncture there occurred a series of incidents which could easily have given the Scots some misgivings concerning English politics in general, and raised uncertainties about their allies, the war party, as well. For Vane and St. John to maintain and even improve their relations with the Scots during a period of general suspicion and doubt took no little amount of skill; yet this is precisely what they succeeded in doing. The events in question were the three separate Royalist plots that came to light in January, all of which were directed against the Covenanters. One involved the city of London; a second, the closest friend of the Scots, Henry Vane; and the third, the religious Independents. All three plots were based on the assumption that the persons being approached opposed Scottish intervention in the war so emphatically that they would desert Parliament and join the Royalists in order to prevent it.

The Brooke plot, first to appear, looked singularly sinister to the Scots. It concerned the city of London and a Papist, Sir Basil Brooke, and consisted of a plan for the Lord Mayor and certain Aldermen to acknowledge the Oxford Parliament (scheduled to meet shortly) as the only true Parliament, and then to present a proposal of peace to the King. The Royalists sent a letter to this effect, signed by Charles and addresesd "to our trusty and well beloved, our Lord Mayor and Aldermen of our City of London and all other our well affected subjects of that city." [45] The incriminating letter managed to be intercepted, and on the 6th of January Vane and St. John presented it to the House of Commons, where it was condemned. Accompanied by Lord Wharton, Vane and St. John then rushed off to give the Scottish commissioners their version of the story. The Scots were shaken by the whole affair. They expected Papists to be mixed up in intrigue, but the implication that the city, the bulwark of Parliament, could be in any way compromised rather distressed them. Another feature of the Brooke plot which especially disturbed the Scots was the suggestion that peace might be made without them.[46] To clear the air, as well their good names, the sheriffs and aldermen of London invited the Scots commissioners to join Parliament and the Assembly of Divines in a banquet. On the day of this sumptuous affair, Stephen Marshall delivered one of his more impressive sermons. The enemy will stop at nothing, he warned, "to divide the City from Parliament, the houses one from another, and the English from the Scots." The only hope for the cause of Parliament–and here Marshall returned to his main theme–was to preserve the unity so necessary to ensure a Royalist defeat.[47]

Even before the reverberations of the Brooke plot subsided, another episode began to unravel. This time Sir Henry Vane, Jr., found himself the recipient of Royalist overtures. The king seemed to be aware that Vane led a sizable and influential party in Parliament, and, unlike the Scots, he knew also that Vane favored religious toleration. On the basis of these two valid premises Charles concluded that once Vane and his "strong party in the house" were promised toleration, they would sue for peace. But the syllogism did not work, simply because not enough information had been supplied. The war party contained men who favored toleration, but it included some who opposed religious liberty as well. Vane may have sided with the former position, but he also saw the necessity of the Scottish alliance, and this kept him from revealing his own preferences. Above all, Vane had been in politics sufficiently long to realize that he could not trust Charles I. When he received a letter from the king's agent, Lord Lovelace, outlining the terms of the proposed treaty, he took it straight to the Scots. He also showed it privately to his associates, St. John, Haselrig, and Samuel Brown, and to the Speaker of the House. But with the Scots, he made a great play of seeking advice.[48] It must have been very flattering for them to be taken into the confidence of the war-party leaders during such a delicate undertaking. Certainly Vane's conduct strengthened their trust, as he skillfully converted an embarrassing offer from the Royalists into political advantage for himself.

The advice given by the Scots was, we may presume, the same as he would have followed in any case: to carry on with the conspirators in the hope that more information might be uncovered. However, before Vane could proceed very far with his counterconspiracy, the Lord General got wind of the correspondence, and without any knowledge of Vane's purpose, accused him of holding intelligence with Oxford, a treasonable offense. Essex's discovery not only cut short the attempt to gather further information, it also led to a dispute between the two houses over a question of Parliamentary privilege. Nothing very much came of the controversy, but the whole episode served to bring the Covenanters even closer to the leaders of the war party.[49]

The last of the conspiracies in this plot-filled month of January centered around the religious Independents. Thomas Ogle, who mistook the Independents for Brownists, thought the two groups shared a common hatred of the Covenanters, and would be willing to support peace in return for toleration. Acting for the Earl of Bristol, an adviser to the king, Ogle approached two Independents, Thomas Goodwin and Philip Nye, with a proposal which even contained an offer to make Nye the king's chaplain. The Ogle plot had as little chance of succeeding as the Lovelace affair, for the Independents had no intention of compromising themselves for some dubious promises. Immediately, Nye and Goodwin informed leading members of Parliament, including this time the Earl of Essex, and they received authorization to continue their correspondence with Ogle; which they did, but nothing more developed.[50] As before, the Scottish commissioners were kept abreast of the various negotiations "in great secrecy, foot by foot as it proceeded."[51] Undoubtedly Vane and St. John acted as informants to the Scots in the Ogle plot, as they had done previously. In any case, the details were presented in such a manner that the Covenanters never publicly or privately accused the Independents of treason, even though Ogle's letters to Nye and Goodwin evidenced some familiarity between them. Furthermore, there is no sign that the Scots even remotely suspected the Independents of any foul play.[52] The fact of the matter remains that Vane and St. John, working closely with the commissioners, had done an extremely effective job of winning their confidence.

In addition to keeping them informed of clandestine activities the war-party leaders inflated the Covenanters' sense of their own importance, confirming their original impression that Scotland was indispensable to the Parliamentary war effort. Moreover, the commissioners became convinced that if prestigious Scottish political figures came to London, the full direction of the war would surely be turned over to them. As early as November 1643 Alexander Henderson wrote from London "That there is a Godly, honest, wise and active committee sent hither, which is much desired by the English, who are perplexed and wearied, and know not what to do, and will be content to be directed by them in all affairs." A month later Baillie repeated the same notion, apparently having gleaned it from his war-party allies. "I cannot but second the earnest desire of all here for the upcoming of a committee from our Estates." He continued:

> It is thought by all our friends that if a well chosen committee were here, they would get the guiding of all the affairs both of this state and church, and without it, the distractions and languishing and fainting of this diseased people will not be cured.[53]

It was true, of course, that the very nature of the alliance between England and Scotland presupposed a joint body which would coordinate strategy and the allocation of resources. This had already been foreseen in the treaty adopted on November 29, 1643: its ninth article mentioned a committee that would be appointed to resolve all differences between the two nations. On the 9th of December a letter received by Parliament from their own commissioners in Edinburgh showed that one of the matters discussed in Scotland had been "Committees of [Both] Kingdoms."[54] Since a joint committee can be considered a logical result of the Anglo-Scottish alliance, the creation of such a body, in one form or another, had the support of practically every member of the English Parliament. Thus when additional Scottish lay commissioners arrived in London on January 31, the stage was set for the establishment of the Committee of Both Kingdoms.[55]

Before the newly arrived commissioners had been given time to rest from their journey, they held a meeting with Vane and St. John concerning the future committee. All of them realized that there could be little delay, for only a day before John Crew had introduced a motion in the House of

Commons calling for the setting up of such a body. A committee of the Commons had been formed for the purpose of framing the enabling legislation.[56] From a war-party point of view, the framework of Crew's measure contained certain important defects. To prevent the undesirable ordinance from passing, Vane and St. John conceived an entirely different approach; but they knew they would have to move quickly. In consultation with the Scots these two drew up a new document, which gave the projected Committee of Both Kingdoms power to order and direct the war as well as authority over settling the terms of the peace. They selected seven Lords and fourteen Commons who would be members of the committee along with the Scottish commissioners, thereby ensuring that the committee would consist of a majority sympathetic to their own aims. If Vane and St. John's bill went through, the militants would gain control over all key matters concerning peace and war. They would also achieve their long-sought-after aim of eclipsing the Lord General.[57]

Unable to introduce their measure into the Commons, where discussion had already begun on Crew's proposal, the war-party leaders decided to present it instead to the House of Lords. The Scots helped the process along by sending a message to the Lords announcing that they brought "instructions to treat with some Commissioners such as Parliament shall appoint, about the managing of the affairs of both Kingdoms." Ironically, their message was read to the Lords by the Earl of Essex, who was seemingly unaware of its implications.[58] Immediately after Essex spoke, Lords Say and Northumberland introduced the ordinance that had been drawn up by Vane and St. John.[59] As now drafted, it provided for an all-powerful committee, one that would "order and direct *whatsoever* doth or may concern the managing of the war." The committee was also given jurisdiction over matters pertaining to the peace of the kingdom, and one clause, general enough to allow unlimited authority, granted it the right to do "*all other things* in pursuance of the ends expressed in the said Covenant and treaty." [60] The list of seven Lords and fourteen Commons devised by Vane and St. John consisted mainly of war-party or ex-middle-party members.[61] Significantly, peace-party adherents Denzil Holles, John Maynard, and the Earl of Pembroke, who had sat on the earlier Committee of Safety, were not included.

Without much excitement or debate, the Lords quickly passed the bill and sent it down to the House of Commons. Whether the Lords were napping, or whether they were too preoccupied with the recruitment of Essex's army, also consideed on this date, we shall never know. But whatever the reason, they seemed eager for the measure to become law. In fact, when they turned it over to the Commons, they requested that the proposal be given "a speedy dispatch in regard to the weight and importance of it." [62]

In the Commons, however, the peace party immediately recognized the implications of the Lords' bill, and the measure encountered considerable opposition. Accounts of the unusual methods used by Vane and St. John had started circulating when Sir William Lewis brought everything out into the open, stating, "It is a way some intend to manage the councils of this house by presenting it first to the Lords and then to present it to us and so to pass things." John Maynard then rose to accuse the Lords of having broken Parliamentary privileges by inserting the names of the Members of the Commons in the projected committee. Here both John Glyn and William Pierrepoint made the observation that there had been precedents for the Lords' procedure. Their position is interesting because it reveals Glyn, a middle-party adherent, and Pierrepoint, formerly of the peace party, as not unsympathetic to the Lords' bill. Holles and Whitelock (now working with the peace group), perhaps realizing that Maynard was pursuing the wrong line of argument, suggested that the Commons return to the original legislation brought in by Crew a few days earlier. At this moment St. John interceded with the point that the Scots favored the Lords' measure and would be extremely disappointed if it did not pass. St. John's admonition had some effect; a committee was appointed "to go to the Scots Commissioners to desire to see their articles so we may draw an order comfortable." [63]

On February 5 the commissioners presented a paper which acquainted Parliament with their powers, and then proceeded to call for the establishment of a method for treating together on a regular basis. The note added: "We are also instructed and warranted to advise and consult with such committees as its Honorable Houses of Parliament shall be pleased to appoint." And it concluded:

> That they would be pleased to lay down some speedy and constant ways of communicating the desires and joining the councils of both Kingdoms, in pursuance of the Covenant, treaty and common interest of his Majesty's two dominions, and for supplying the present necessities of these armies.[64]

However, despite the efforts of the Scots, a majority of the lower house chose to put aside the Lords' ordinance; and on February 7 the house turned once again to Crew's proposal.[65] The legislation which emerged, after much debate, differed from that sent from the upper house in curtailing the power of the new committee considerably. It would still possess authority to order and direct the management of the war, but would be allowed to deal only in an advisory capacity with matters regarding the ends expressed in the Covenant and treaty. Furthermore, the committee was denied jurisdiction over peace negotiations, a point clearly spelled out so as to avoid any ambivalence:

> Provided always that nothing in this ordinance shall authorize the Committee hereby appointed to advise, treat or consult, concerning any cessation of arms, or making peace without express directions from both houses of Parliament.

Finally, in order to restrict its mandate still further, the Commons granted the committee only three months' tenure; whereas the committee proposed by Vane and St. John set no time limit on its duration.[66]

Only one matter remained to be discussed: the selection of members to serve on the committee. A recommendation was made to accept the original list of names sent down by the Lords on February 1; but this suggestion met with the immediate disapproval of the peace group, who, as we pointed out earlier, were underrepresented on this list. They asked for additional members to be added, and their motion led to a lengthy debate and a division, Holles and Lewis acting as tellers for the peace group, Haselrig and Vane for the militants. With a margin of fourteen the designated names went through, constituting a defeat for the peace party.[67] But for whom was this actually a victory?

The original war-party measure devised by Vane and St. John failed even to warrant a division, which indicated that a large majority in the Commons opposed the bill. On the other hand, a majority was at the same time content to accept the very same names chosen for the proposed committee by these two men. Assuming that both peace- and war-party supporters voted with their respective groups on the foregoing issues, then the conclusion is inescapable that there existed a body of unaligned Members of Parliament who shifted sides on the two votes. These consisted for the most part of M.P.s who had belonged to Pym's middle party. We know, for example, that Sir Gilbert Gerrard and John Glyn, two former associates of Pym, backed the final version of the ordinance establishing the Committee of Both Kingdoms, and there is good reason to believe that Sir John Clotworthy went along with them.[68]

The maneuvering in the House of Commons, with the salvaging of one important feature of the war-party bill, seems to suggest the operating of a compromise solution. And the likely person to have brought it about was Oliver St. John, whose contacts with the middle group could now be turned to advantage. St. John and Vane must have seen that without support from men in the middle, there could be no hope for forming anything resembling a powerful committee. St. John's willingness to compromise in order to achieve his purpose had already been demonstrated on February 3, when he had announced that he shared certain objections to aspects of the Lords' ordinance, and felt that it should be sent to committee.[69] The significance of his statement is obvious: the bill which he now proposed to revise was the one which he himself had helped to draft. But he doubtless realized that those sympathetic to a middle-group policy under Pym, and still uncommitted to either the peace or the war parties, would be more apt to give their approval to the final, more moderate, version of the legislation.[70]

They knew as well as St. John that a Committee of Both Kingdoms was essential for good relations with the Scots, and would create a more efficient instrument for marshaling the resources of the two countries. By setting up a committee with executive functions, a way might be found to eliminate the squabble over military leadership that had marked the last six months. These men, opposed to both extremes, had seen how, only a month previously, a serious disagreement between Essex and Waller rocked the House of Commons. Recriminations had been cast about and threats of resignation made, all of which could only serve to weaken Parliamentary unity. At the time, a temporary settlement had been arrived at when Sir Walter Earle devised a compromise.[71] Members who shared Earle's viewpoint and were anxoius to avoid disunity wherever possible would support a Committee of Both Kingdoms, which could take over the direction of the war and remove responsibility for military planning from the individual generals. With a Parliamentary committee in control of operations, the generals would be able to go on with the business of war and leave politics to the politicians.

It is interesting to note, in this regard, that those who still held a middle-party position were fairly well represented on the Committee of Both Kingdoms. For, in addition to Gerrard and Glyn, there were three others who had been sympathetic to a middle way. The Earl of Manchester had been a leader of the middle group in the Lords, and his later rather checkered career can be explained as adherence to a middle-party outlook when such an approach to politics was no longer tenable.[72] John Crew and William Pierrepoint were described by Clarendon as two moderates who by early 1645 had contracted bitterness toward the king. Crew, as we know, introduced the first proposal for a Committee of Both Kingdoms; while Pierrepoint, although favoring the establishment of the committee, had shown surprise at his name appearing on the list of members that the Lords sent down, the one drawn up by Vane and St. John. The senior Henry Vane, although frequently viewed as an appendage to his influential son, nevertheless opposed him at various times, so he must be considered, a neutral.[73] With only one person away fighting (Manchester), the noncommitted had five permanent representatives on the committee. This may not seem significant on a council of twenty-one men, but the peace party had even fewer supporters to speak for them. The latter group would have only one out of three (Stapleton) always in attendance, since the Earls of Essex and Warwick had to devote their full energies to the war.[74]

The war party, combining "fiery spirits" and militant former middle-party members, had twelve on the committee. These included, from the Commons: Sir William Waller, who spoke of himself as belonging to the godly at this time; Sir William Armine, a close associate of Vane; Sir Arthur Haselrig; Robert Wallop; Oliver Cromwell; Samuel Brown; St. John; and Vane himself.[75] The lords were Lord Robartes, Lord Wharton, Lord Say, and the Earl of Northumberland, the last three being closely associated with the Covenanters at this time.[76] However, out of this total of twelve, four would be away with the army (Robartes, Cromwell, Haselrig, and Waller) and one (Armine) on a permanent mission to the north.

Thus the war party, with seven active representatives, had a clear majority: and when their total is added to the four Scottish commissioners, it is obvious that the Committee of Both Kingdoms rested safely in the hands of a coalition of Scots and English militants. It is no wonder, then, that on February 7 Holles and Lewis attempted to have more peace-party representatives added. Defeated in the Commons, they next tried to convince Essex that the ordinance establishing the committee was directed solely at him and would serve to curtail his authority. Baillie wrote that Holles and his associates "did work on the facility of the General, providing him with demonstrations of his limitation and degradation by this Committee."[77]

On the 10th of February the Lords sent four proposals to the Commons, all of which aimed at weakening the power of the committee and changing the political complexion of its membership. The Lords held that the words "order and direct," in regard to regulating the management of the war, should be omitted. Another amendment sought to restrict the committee to acting on instructions given to them regularly by Parliament. A third revision called for the raising of the quorum from six to nine, while the final one would have enlarged the committee so as to include a number of peace-inclined Lords. The Commons rejected these amendments in very short order,[78] but tempers at the conference must have been frayed because Edmund Prideaux was prodded into revealing the war party's motive, i.e., reducing the Lord General's autonomy. Prideaux put it rather bluntly: "Without such a Committee," he warned, "the war will be carried on without the Two houses."[79] (Vane had actually made the same point in the Commons on February 9, when he had declared that supreme military power ought always to reside with Parliament instead of with the generals.[80])

As a result of Prideaux's admission, the Lords began to argue that the committee as now constituted would remove the "active part" of the war from the Lord General's control, thereby diminishing his just authority.[81] But the Commons persisted in their efforts to get the bill passed as it stood, and for a time it appeared that the two houses might be hopelessly divided. On February 16, after days of wrangling, the Lords finally decided to accept the ordinance in its unaltered form. Their capitulation came, however, only after the Earl of Essex gave his consent. Here we can see another example of the Lord General's dedication to the Parliamentary cause, which he knew must suffer considerable damage if the dispute continued.[82] Essex took the step of resolving the impasse even though he realized that his own power would be diminished by the Committee of Both Kingdoms. He accepted his fate, as Dewes observed, and received "much discontent and discouragement." [83]

Yet undoubtedly another factor played a role in convincing the Lords to relent, and this had to do with the pressure applied by the Scots. Repeatedly, in conferences with the upper house, the Commons insisted that the Scots were growing impatient with Parliament, and that the alliance between the two countries would deteriorate if the ordinance failed to pass. Prideaux had this in mind when he asked the Lords at a conference "to expedite this business, for the Scottish Commissioners who traveled long hours and done nothing, might have some contributions to write to the Scottish army." [84] The Scots, for their part, aided their own cause by writing to Parliament and reminding them of the dangers of delay: "The enemy is restless and vigilant, and will neglect no opportunities." [85] Baillie seemed to think that their letters carried the day. "We gave a short and sharp enough paper to both houses," he wrote,

> to be at a point, if they thought meet to make any use of our Committee, which so oft and so earnestly they had sought for. It was so guided, that the Commons unanimously agreed to the former ordinance, and required the Lords to stand to their own side.[86]

Mercurius Aulicus hit the mark when it taunted Parliament's supporters with: "Notwithstanding all this [opposition] the high Court of Committees must go; for the Scots Commissioners will have it so." [87]

The emergence of the Committee of Both Kingdoms resulted from the cooperation between the militants and the Scots. The war-party leaders had been convinced for a long time that with Essex in control of military affairs, Parliament would never win the war. By creating a body that superseded his authority and was unsympathetic to his position in matters of peace and war, they now believed victory could be achieved. The Scots expressed the same view. "If this [Committee of Both Kingdoms] were passed," they declared, "we look for new life and vigor in all affairs." Thus when the ordinance was finally made law the Scots regarded this enactment as a victory for themselves; "fully according to our mind," as Baillie noted.[88] But in reality it has to be viewed as a triumph for the war party, which had increased their influence at the expense of their rivals. As Denzil Holles realized, they had, through their majority on the committee, "engrossed the whole managing of war," and from his vantage point, "this was the first step of those unworthy men getting into power." [89]

NOTES

1. See Introduction, above.
2. C.S.P. Ven., pp. 32, 47, 52.
3. C.S. Terry, ed., *Paper Relating to the Army of the Solemn League and Covenant* (Edinburgh, 1917), pp. X-XI.
4. C.S.P. Ven., p. 53.
5. For the following I rely heavily on J. H. Hexter, *The Reign of King Pym,* op. cit.
6. It would seem to me that Professor John R. MacCormack, in his recent book, *Revolutionary Politics in the Long Parliament* (Cambridge, Mass., 1973), p. 12, exaggerates the extremism of the war party, whom he calls anachronistically, "radicals." A few loose words about

republicanism got Henry Marten thrown into the Tower for quite a few years. For further comments on this book, see my review in *Science and Society,* XL (1976).

7. Hexter, p. 70. Dr. Pearl believes that the middle group had possibly as few as fifteen active members. See "Oliver St. John and the 'middle group' in the Long Parliament," *English Historical Review,* LXXXI (1966), p. 494, n. 1.
8. Ibid., pp. 56-57. As were at various times Glyn, Clotworthy, and Whitelock.
9. Baillie, II, p. 483; see also David Buchanan, *Truth Its Manifest* (London, 1645), p. 51.
10. Lawrence Kaplan, op. cit.
11. *Parliament of Scotland,* VI, p. 70.
12. *Register of Instructions to the Scots Commission in London, 1644-1646,* MSS in General Register House, Edinburgh. Henceforth cited as *Instructions.*
13. Baillie, II, p. 154. "We wonder your ambassadors should be dreaming of any treaty."
14. This analysis differs from Dr. Pearl, op. cit., who maintains that the middle party continued for one more year. Further proof for my position will come out in the course of this chapter.
15. Baillie, II, p. 216.
16. Clarendon, III, pp. 216-217; See also Violet Rowe, op. cit.
17. Denzil Lord Holles, *Memoris* (London, 1699), p. 14.
18. See e.g., C.J. III, p. 350; Dewes, 165, fol. 213v.
19. D.N.B.; Clarendon, III, p. 332; Hexter, p. 168.
20. Clarendon, II, p. 78; III, p. 183.
21. *Thurloe State Papers,* I, p. 75; John Nicholls (ed.), *Original Letters and Papers of State, Addressed to Oliver Cromwell* (London, 1743), pp. 24-25. Valerie Pearl, op. cit., p. 500.
22. Baillie, II, pp. 133, 135. Dr. Violet A. Rowe believes that Vane and St. John combined to lead the war party after Pym's death, op. cit., p. 34. Dr. Valerie Pearl, on the other hand, argues that St. John continued to act as leader of the middle party well into 1644. Yet St. John's willingness to work so closely with Vane on so many matters would

seem to indicate an alliance outside the middle group. Thus in January 1644 Essex, a general whom Dr. Pearl links with the middle party, charged both Vane and St. John of "high treason for holding intelligence with Oxford" (Baillie, II, p. 135). Moreover, Dr. Pearl offers no concrete proof that St. John worked in favor of Essex. Her one example of how St. John called for a compromise in a dispute concerning the Lord General on January 1, 1644, op. cit., p. 508, is somewhat ambiguous, as Dewes's version of St. John's speech can be interpreted as criticism of Essex. Dewes, 165, fols. 266-266v.

23. T.T., E. 338 (1).
24. Lawrence Whitacre, *Diary of the Proceedings in the House of Commons,* B.M., Add. MSS, 31,116, fols. 167, 172.
25. T.T., E. 74 (7).
26. Dewes, 165, fol. 213v.
27. For a fuller discussion of the religious truce, see: Lawrence Kaplan, "Presbyterians and Independents in 1643," *English Historical Review,* LXXXIV (1969), pp. 244-256.
28. Baillie, II, pp. 117-119.
29. Buchanan, p. 54.
30. Gardiner, *Civil War,* I, p. 20.
31. Richard Baxter, *Reliquae Baxterianae* (London, 1696), p. 47.
32. Hexter, chaps. VII and VIII, passim.
33. L.J., VI, p. 377.
34. Dewes, 165, fol. 223v.
35. Ibid., fols. 228v-230; C.J., III, p. 370. The matter was referred to a committee and Holland was finally acquitted.
36. Ibid., fol. 223v. See also J. H. Hexter, "The Rise of the Independent Party," unpublished thesis, Harvard University, 1936. Dr. Pearl, making light of this incident, argues that Stapleton continued to be a member of the middle group (op. cit., pp. 494n, 512n); but this ignores his voting pattern as well as the impression of contemporaries such as Baillie, who in January 1644 spoke of "Sir Philip Stapleton, Mr. Holles and others of the General's party" (II, p. 136).
37. Holles in his *Memoirs,* trying to excuse this delay, mentions how

others supposedly formented differences between Essex and himself (pp. 13-14).

38. Ibid.
39. Dr. Lotte Glow, in her article "Pym and Parliament, The Methods of Moderation," *Journal of Modern History* (1964), pp. 373-397, agrees with Dewes that there was a split, with Vane representing northerners and Prideaux representing the west-country men (p. 387).
40. For Strode, see Dewes, 165, fol. 213v; for Haselrig, see Yonge, 18,779, fol. 5; for Prideaux, see Dewes, 165, fol. 233v; for Wentworth, see *ibid.,* fol. 226v; for Trenchard, see ibid., fol. 233v. Trenchard escaped to the army in 1647 and was a Rumper.
41. C.J., VI, pp. 308, 350, 370, 391, 414, 424, 427, 443, 458.
42. Baillie, II, pp. 112-114.
43. Ibid., pp. 118-119. It would have been nearly impossible for St. John to favor Essex openly and be on good terms with the Scots at this time. Nor does it seem likely that their impression of Essex could have come from moderates.
44. Ibid., p. 483, p. 187. The Scots also accepted the war party's account of the Holland affair (ibid., p. 135).
45. *Camden Miscellany,* vol. VIII, pp. V-VI.
46. *Baillie,* II, p. 133.
47. T.T., E. 29 (3); T.T., E. 30 (2).
48. Baillie, II, pp. 135-136; Bulstrode Whitelock, *Memorials of the English Affairs,* 4 vols. (Oxford, 1853), II, p. 235.
49. Baillie, II, p. 135-136.
50. Whitelock, II, p. 236; C.J., VI, p. 378.
51. Baillie, p. 137.
52. Ibid., pp. 135-137.
53. Ibid., pp. 483-484; pp. 106-107.
54. Rushworth, II, p. 487; C.J., VI, p. 335.
55. The three commissioners appointed were Warriston, Loudoun, and Robert Barclay, and they were joined by Maitland. All four of them were at this time in sympathy with the Argyll party in Scotland. Loudoun does not appear to have made the trip at this time.

56. Yonge, 18,779, fol. 56; C.J., VI, p. 382.
57. Baillie, II, p. 141. Professor Wallace Notestein, quoting the same passage, suggests that it was the Scots who originated the ordinance. See "The Establishment of the Committee of Both Kingdoms," *American Historical Review* (1912), p. 482. Although Baillie's language is not quite precise here, it appears to this reader that he does indicate that Vane and St. John drew up the measure. He wrote: "When we [the Scots] had agreed with Sir Henry Vane and the Solicitor upon the draft . . . ." Also, the selection of the twenty-one names for the committee would hardly have been the work of newly arrived foreigners.
58. L.J., VI, p. 405. Although Essex read the letter, it cannot necessarily be assumed that he supported the measure. However, the fact that it was passed so rapidly by the Lords indicates that Essex took no steps to prevent its passage.
59. Yonge, 18,779, fol. 61.
60. *Acts and Ordinances,* I, pp. 436-437 (italics added).
61. See below, pp. 23-25.
62. C.J., III, p. 384; L.J., VI, p. 407.
63. Yonge, 18,779, fol. 61.
64. L.J., VI, p. 410.
65. Dewes, 166, fol. 9. Professor Notestein does not seem to realize that the final measure stemmed from Crew's proposal.
66. *Acts and Ordinances,* I, pp. 381-382. Notestein believed that this measure gave the committee power to treat (op. cit., p. 488).
67. C.J., III, p. 391.
68. For Glyn, see Yonge, 18,779, fol. 61; he also supported the renewal measure in May (Dewes, 166, fol. 616). For Gerrard, see Dewes, 166, fol. 146, and in May ibid., p. 616. Clotworthy was selected to bring the ordinance up to the Lords on February 3, and was teller in support of the May ordinance (C.J., III, pp. 387, 483).
69. Yonge, 18,779, fol. 61.
70. Dr. Pearl believes that St. John's willingness to compromise is evidence that he still led the middle group at this time. To prove that

he preferred moderate solutions, she conjectures about his motive: "... it is more than likely that he was unhappy from the start about the original draft, but was outnumbered by Vane and the Scots" (op. cit., p. 509). Yet this is to minimize his role in the maneuver which sent the measure for a powerful committee through the House of Lords, a somewhat unique approach, revealing St. John's experienced hand rather than that of the less influential Vane. Moreover, the Scots never criticized St. John for his compromise, indicating that tactics and not belief played a greater role with him.

71. Dewes, fol. 233v.
72. Hexter, p. 88; *D.N.B.*
73. Clarendon, III, p. 497; for Pierrepoint, see Yonge, 18,779, fol. 61; Dewes, 166, fol. 7; for Henry Vane Sr., see Dewes, 115, fol. 213v.
74. Warwick associated with the peace party at about the time of the incident concerning his brother, the Earl of Holland; Baillie, II, p. 135. Even Stapleton had a military commission.
75. For Waller, see Waller, op. cit., pp. 5-6; for Armine, see *D.N.B.;* for Browne, St. John's close associate, see Whitelock, II, pp. 466-467; for Wallop, see C.J., IV, pp. 125, 214. The others have already been discussed.
76. For Northumberland, see Baillie, who says, "My Lord Northumberland joining effectively with all our desires, our army now being master of his lands" (II, p. 141). For Wharton, see ibid., p. 133, for Say, see Holles's sarcastic remark regarding his relationship to the Earl of Essex, *Memoris,* p. 12, and Baillie, II, p. 141. For Robartes, Clarendon tells us that he was, at this time "in great conjunction with Sir H. Vane [Jr.]," III, pp. 386-387.
77. Baillie, II, p. 141.
78. C.J., III, p. 395; L.J., IV, pp. 421-422.
79. L.J., VI, p. 423.
80. Yonge, 18,779, fol. 64v.
81. L.J., VI, p. 423.
82. C.J., III, p. 401; L.J., VI, p. 427. He was to perform a similar magnanimous service when he resigned his commission a year later.

83. Dewes, 166, fol. 136.
84. Ibid., fol. 10v.
85. L.J., VI, p. 417.
86. Baillie, II, p. 141.
87. *Mercurius Aulicus,* February 10, 1644. This was a Royalist journal.
88. Baillie, II, p. 141.
89. Holles, pp. 5-6.

II

A Breach in the Coalition

On February 16 the ordinance appointing a Committee of Both Kingdoms became law. It represented, as we saw, a victory for the coalition of war party and Covenanters. During the next few months this coalition was further strengthened, unquestionably to the mutual advantage of both parties. Yet barely seven months after the February ordinance, the alliance fell to pieces, leaving the Scots stunned and disoriented. By the following year a Royalist newsbook could congratulate itself because of an earlier prediction:

> We told you this time twelvemonth when the Scots invaded England that those who fetched them in (before the year expired) would as earnestly wish them out, which is now so true.[1]

But in February 1644 the Scottish commissioners had no premonition of those future developments, which would turn their firmest allies into their bitterest opponents. At this time the existence of a close association with the militants appeared to be a most satisfactory arrangement, as their partners looked after Scottish needs and interests. That they performed this function faithfully was begrudgingly admitted by one Scotsman who later became very critical of the war party. Its leaders, he wrote in 1645,

> did endear themselves unto the Scots by sundry good offices for a time, which they did unto them in things concerning their forces in England and Ireland, employed in the common service, and by their constant and frequent courting of the Scots.[2]

Of all the members of Parliament, Sir Henry Vane, Jr., remained the most concerned with Scottish requirements. The diaries for early 1644 reveal him as a consistent advocate of causes favorable to them. For example, on February 26:

> Sir Henry Vane, Jr. made report from the Scottish Commissioners of the want of their army in Ireland and the non-payment of their army here, and that some speedy course must be taken for they could not any longer continue with words.

On that day the House of Commons agreed to accept Vane's plan for the payment of the Scots, whereby "a tax should be laid upon the northern counties . . . and that they should have the sequestration of the north and the benefit of the coal." [3] On April 8, and again on April 27th, he spoke out in favor of aid to the Scottish army. And well into the summer of 1644, we find Vane reminding the lower house about "great arrears due to the Scots, and [he] showed that the Scottish army in the north needed vast sums and desired us to think of some way of paying them." [4]

The Scots traditionally maintained a strong interest in Ireland. Upon their insistence, Vane managed to secure agreement by the Commons to a clause in the November 28 treaty placing English troops in Ireland under the command of a Scottish general. Three and one-half months later, on March 9, 1644, the Lords resolved that "the British and Scottish forces in Ireland shall be under one Commander in Chief," carrying the implication of Scottish control. Finally, on the 11th of April the upper house specified

> that the Earl of Leven, Lord General of the Scots forces in Ieland being now, by the votes of both houses, agreed to be Commander in Chief over all forces, as well British as Scots.[5]

It was in the area of military affairs within England that the goals of the Covenanters and the war party most strongly coincided. The formation of the Committee of Both Kingdoms seemed a perfect solution, in that it reduced the autonomy of the general whom the Scots did not trust, by giving to this body power over the organization, recruitment, and provisioning of the various Parliamentary armies, Scottish as well as English. But most important, it allowed those who controlled the committee to oversee strategy for the war itself. The Scottish commissioners obviously wanted the committee established for these reasons, as well as the fact that they were now provided with a ready-made vehicle to influence English politics. Indeed, through the Committee of Both Kingdoms the Scots obtained a greater voice in military and political matters than their own contribution warranted. It is therefore understandable why various contemporaries referred to the committee as "the Scottish Committee";[6] and natural enough that the Scots would use every possible means to help the war party in their efforts to extend the competence of this new executive organ.

When in February 1644 the war party's original request for an omnipotent committee failed to gain the support of the Commons, the militants seemed to be checked in achieving their ambitions. But once the committee started taking shape, other possibilities for expanding its mandate presented themselves.

The first steps taken by the committee, essential to its functioning, met with no opposition. Thus it was announced that meetings would be held in Derby House every afternoon, and subcommittees were formed for the purpose of drafting and receiving letters from all Parliamentary armies. The generals of these armies received requests to send messages describing each day's activities, "whether the posture of affairs do require it or not." The committee created posts in different parts of the country to facilitate the gathering of intelligence, as it wanted to be in a position to learn immediately the changing needs of the armies. Finally, the sum of £300 per week was listed as an operating fund for intelligence work.[7] Straightforward measures like the foregoing encountered no resistance. But other proposals designed to strengthen the Committee of Both Kingdoms evoked an immediate negative response, and set off controversies lasting for months.

When the Lords approved the final ordinance creating the committee they added two qualifications that were to act as restraints. First they stated that if the Lord General received an order from the Committee of Both Kingdoms that he found unacceptable, he might ignore the command and appeal to Parliament to have it revoked. Second, the Lords declared that every peer had the right to attend meetings at Derby House.[8] This second proviso would make it impossible to keep the sessions secret and would allow moderate Lords, not originally chosen, to come to each meeting for the purpose of influencing decisions. Nevertheless, the first qualification was viewed as more threatening; for if effectuated, it would have removed the committee from any real control over Parliament's most important army, thereby restoring to the Lord General that very authority which had just been reduced. In essence these two reservations taken together would make the ordinance for an executive committee of Both Kingdoms a dead letter. It is therefore not surprising that the war party and their allies aimed to remove the Lords' clauses without delay.[9]

On the 20th of February the Commons passed an ordinance calling on all members of the committee to take an oath of secrecy.[10] In addition to establishing the principle that members could discuss matters of state *in camera* without fear of having their views disclosed, this measure plainly intended to exclude from committee meetings all members of Parliament, Lords and Commons alike, not specifically called upon to participate. The Lords, however, refused to agree to the oath, and managed to put off accepting the principle of secrecy until July 1644, when, as we note below, they had no choice but to accede.[11]

Though temporarily delayed in regard to the question of secrecy, the militant members met with a greater measure of success in their efforts to eliminate all ambiguities regarding Essex's chain of command. In order to accomplish this goal they had to overcome the objections of Sir Philip Stapleton, John Glyn, and other former members of the middle group who endeavored to maintain the Lord General's autonomy.[12] But here the war-party leaders held a trump card in reserve, which they now threatened to use. If the Lords and Commons would not agree to the provision that Essex was subject to the Committee of Both Kingdoms without any right of appeal, they would obstruct the recruitment and financing of the Lord General's army. He would be an independent general, but without any army to command. Faced with this eventuality Essex's supporters bowed to necessity. On March 26 "an ordinance for the speedy completing and maintaining of the army under the immediate command of Robert, Earl of Essex," was enacted, with the provision that the Lord General "shall be subject to the orders and directions of both houses of Parliament or the Committee of both Kingdoms." [13]

It is clear that the buttressing of the Committee of Both Kingdoms met with the enthusiastic approval of the Covenanters. Whenever possible, the Scottish commissioners entered Parliamentary controversies in order to influence an outcome favorable to themselves. Thus in May 1644, when the Lords decided to utilize the opportunity presented by the conclusion of the Committee's allotted tenure to suggest revisions in its mandate, the Scots immediately intervened. The Lords sought to alter the membership of the commiteee for the very obvious purpose of changing its political complexion. The Scots interpreted the attempt to bring in new members as a direct threat to their country's interests. They saw the same men who had originally opposed the establishment of a joint committee now seeking to reduce the Scots' proportionate strength, as well as to dilute the militancy of the committee itself. Some Scots imagined that even more sinister designs were afoot. Baillie had the impression that the addition of peace-party men "might have overswayed the better party and us," and he feared that the Lord's measure would transform the committee to such an extent "that it should be an engine against us." [14]

Baillie's trepidations might have been somewhat overdrawn. What seems more probable is that when the Committee of Both Kingdoms came to be renewed, Essex and his associates in the peace party sought to neutralize the preponderant influence of the "violents." These members, whom the Lords now suggested, were unquestionably some of the most pacific in Parliament. Denzil Holles headed their list of names, followed by the Earl of Pembroke and others of a similar stamp. The war party met the proposed additions with the dubious claim that the Lords had broken the lower house's privilege by naming members of the Commons in their ordinance. They made the assertion even though the procedure they now criticized had previously been employed by them in a similar situation in February.[15] Fortunately, no one pursued the constitutional question on this later occasion, for the discussion might have revealed embarrassing inconsistencies. The war party did not need to press the issue of privilege either, because a large majority in the Commons, including a group of ex-middle-party men led by Gerrard, Glyn, Crew, Mildmay, and even Clotworthy, supported their contention that the Committee of Both Kingdoms should be renewed in its present form.[16]

The Lords refused to be swayed and stuck to their guns throughout the month of May, demonstrating that they would prefer the committee to lapse (as it did on May 16) rather than permit the war party to maintain its domination. The Lords calculated that the Commons would accept their revisions rather than have no committee at all, and therefore they remained intransigent. But they calculated incorrectly. By refusing to renew the ordinance, the Lords demonstrated to the Commons a willingness to play politics with a crucial military issue: without the Committee of Both Kingdoms, Parliament would no longer have an executive agency capable of directing the war. In addition, their Scottish allies would be unable to hold "the good correspondence" with Parliament that was a sine qua non of the alliance itself.[17] Apparently the Lords' unyielding attitude convinced a majority in the Commons that drastic measures must be taken, for the matter was turned over to some of the most militant members of the Commons to be handled in the manner they saw fit.[18]

The first step was to call upon the City of London to put pressure on the Lords. On the very day that the Committee of Both Kingdoms expired, a petition arrived in Parliament from the City requesting the Lords to continue the committee "as the present exigents of affairs require." [19] With good reason the peace party viewed this petition as having been "set on foot by those who were not his [Essex's] friends." [20] The Lords reacted to this early sign of pressure by calling for a compromise solution. If the Commons would consent to an expanded committee the Lords would agree to name only the additional peers, leaving the lower house free to decide on the new members from the Commons. This offer did not give away very much, and the Commons chose to ignore it. The Lords had waited too long.

On May 22 the militant William Strode suggested that an extraordinary course of action be taken. He moved that the original bill sent from the Lords on February 1, 1644, the one drawn up by St. John and Vane, which had created a committee with unlimited authority, should now be resurrected and put into effect. The Commons, Strode argued, was entitled to revive this measure since the motion had never been acted upon, but had been put aside. Technically the Lords had already registered their approval when they sent the measure to the Commons over three months earlier.[21]

Now revived in its previously unacceptable form, the motion carried by ninety-five votes to fifty-two, a majority of forty-three, a figure three times as great as the margin received by the compromise ordinance in February.[22] The protests of peace-party members Maynard, Whitelock, and Reynolds proved unavailing. Circumvented in this unusual manner, the Lords had to sit by helplessly while an omnipotent Committee of Both Kingdoms resumed command of Parliament's forces. They could hardly console themselves with the sop thrown them on the 24th of May, when the Commons agreed to limit the life of the committee to four months.[23]

The fact that the war party carried the Commons along with them on this occasion raises an important question: Why did such a large proportion of the lower house accept in May a measure that they had rejected in February? For at that time, as we saw, the original war-party ordinance was dismissed without even necessitating a division. A possible answer can be found in the Parliamentary diary of Lawrence Whitacre, member from Okehampton in Devonshire. Whitacre's diary is generally of limited value to historians of Parliamentary politics, chiefly because he tended to restrict himself to an objective reporting of ordinances suggested and passed, committees appointed, etc., but omitted the debates and the persons involved in them. In other words, Whitacre's account of Parliamentary affairs differs little from the dull and formal record in the Parliamentary journals. Nevertheless, on May 22 Whitacre made an offhand observation concerning the renewal of the Committee of Both Kingdoms, which reveals the consensus reached by unaligned members. He wrote that although the legislation did grant "too vast a power," yet

> in this great and pressing necessity in which the Kingdom was involved we should want the service of that Committee, which was absolutely necessary, that the delaying of it any longer might be our ruin.[24]

Thus a majority of the Commons were quite prepared to back almost any measure that they regarded as essential for the effective prosecution of the war (in this case the avoidance of military anarchy). The attitude of these neutral members, once gleaned, allows us to understand how the war party could obtain Parliamentary support for radical policies.

Lawrence Whitacre may not have viewed the renewal of the Committee of Both Kingdoms as a partisan device, but others, and especially the Scots, certainly saw it this way. "The Oxfordian faction is now quieter here," wrote Baillie in his description of how "By God's providence" the committee was sustained.[25] The war party must have been as jubilant as the Scots, but they recognized the limitations of their success. In order to assure the passage of "the omnipotent ordinance," the only measure that could have permitted the Committee of Both Kingdoms to continue under the circumstances, the war-party leaders undoubtedly gave assurances that they would act with restraint.

While there is nothing concrete to substantiate this claim, certain subsequent events seem to indicate that promises had been made to calm the fears of neutrals. For instance, an examination of the committee's letter book after May 22, 1644 shows that, although possessing greater authority, the committee did not act any differently from before; nor did it assume any of the new powers granted by the May ordinance. There is, moreover, no evidence to demonstrate that contemporaries believed the Committee of Both Kingdoms acted more aggressively than previously. An additional proof is the fact that the committee was again renewed two months later, in July, rather than after its allotted four months' tenure. And in the ordinance of July, the mandate of the committee became once more what it had been in the modified version of February 16: only a specified authority. There was just one new addition to the July ordinance: members of the committee would now have to swear an oath of secrecy.[26] This would seem to have been the price the Lords were required to pay for their obstinacy in May.

The militants succeeded in retaining the Committee of Both Kingdoms and generally in furthering the war effort, because they had the backing of a majority of the Commons. Throughout 1644, whatever measures were needed to strengthen Parliament's military posture, the war party could be reasonably certain of easy passage. But this support quickly dissolved when the "violent spirits" turned their attention to the question of devising a treaty with the king. That the war party should take the initiative in seeking peace seems almost a contradiction in terms, as one of their central tenets was that no treaty could possibly be contemplated until such time as Charles admitted defeat on the field of battle. Furthermore, during the first year and one-half of the war they had obstructed every effort Parliament had made for peace. And yet in the spring of 1644 the war party, more than any other, prepared the way for the next peace treaty (the Treaty of Uxbridge). How did this apparent *volte face* come about?

The answer lay in the relationship between the Scots and their allies. The leaders of the war party never altered their attitude regarding negotiations with the king. But the necessities of their alliance demanded that they give the Scots free rein, and the Scots wanted to become peacemakers. Almost every time the Estates in Edinburgh sent commissioners to London they included the advice: "Don't neglect any opportunity for peace." [27] When the first strictly lay delegation of Scotsmen arrived in London in January 1644, they informed Parliament that the time was ripe for a settlement.[28] Immediately after the creation of the Committee of Both Kingdoms, the Scots expressed strong disappointment at the committee's incapacity to arrange for cessation of hostilities. On the very day following passage of the enabling ordinance by the Lords, the Scots complained to Parliament that, while they had instructions from their nation "to save effusion of blood, the Committee had no power to treat of peace." [29]

During the next few months the Scottish commissioners attempted to gain for the joint committee a major role in negotiating peace. They were aided by the king, who decided that a pacific gesture on his part at this time might strengthen his hand. On March 3 Charles sent a letter to London calling on Parliament "to meet with his representatives in order to settle the present distractions of this our Kingdom, and to procure a happy peace." [30] On the advice of the Commons, and without any objections from the

Lords, it was decided to have the Committee of Both Kingdoms prepare an answer to the king's letter. This body was ideally suited for a task of this sort, since the Scots, acting within the committee, could offer their advice during the forming of the reply.[31] There seemed to be nothing particularly revolutionary about giving such an assignment to the Committee of Both Kingdoms, for the matter at hand appeared to be routine and relatively insignificant. Yet almost unobserved, a precedent had been set which would be followed up very shortly.

On March 9 Parliament issued the joint committee's reply to the king's letter, and six days later the House of Commons resolved

> that it be referred to the Committee of Both Kingdoms to consider of, and prepare some grounds for settling a just and safe peace in all his Majesty's dominions such as both Kingdoms may consent unto and prosecute, and to present them to both houses.[32]

In the Commons the foregoing resolution slipped through without engendering any controversy. However, in the upper house it encountered an immediate adverse reaction, and for good reason. The Lords refused to turn over peace negotiations to any agency whose leading members favored the prolongation of the war. Knowing that they could hardly trust "violent spirits" to devise terms congenial to the king, the House of Lords proposed instead the formation of an entirely new committee whose only function would be the framing of a treaty. In spite of pressure from the Commons, the peers persisted in this plan.[33]

The disagreement between the houses showed every sign of developing into a long-drawn-out affair, presenting the prospect that proposals for peace might be delayed indefinitely. This eventuality did not greatly disturb the war party, who were content to go through the motions for the benefit of their Scottish allies, without actually striving to bring peace any nearer. But on March 20 a new factor was introduced. For on that day the Dutch ambassador delivered a message offering his services as a mediator between the king and his Parliament. The ambassador's friendly gesture reopened the question of peacemaking, and the Lords immediately moved that a separate committte be named to consider the Dutch offer. The war-party leaders again reiterated their stock retort to matters concerning such negotiations: the Committee of Both Kingdoms was best equipped to draw up proposals, and besides, any new committee would greatly inconvenience Parliament's Scottish allies.[34]

While the militants directed their attention to answering the Lords, the leaders of the peace party, men like Holles, Stapleton, and Clotworthy, began taking the initiative for themselves. They made contact with noncommitted members of the Commons who sincerely wished to bring about cessation of arms. Their object was to get the Commons to join with the Lords in working constructively for peace, and they made the valid point that a committee dominated by militants could not be relied upon to draw up an equitable treaty, one that Charles would be able to accept.[35] It will be recalled that in February, when the mandate of the committee came under discussion, a majority of the Commons refused to entrust it with jurisdiction over peace negotiations. Those M.P.s who opposed granting this power to the committee in February must have had serious reservations about a decision to bestow the same power a month later.

The appeal for a second committee evoked a noticeable response. When the Lords proposed for the third time that a special body be created to join with nine Lords in considering the Dutch ambassador's proposals, Sir Philip Stapleton called for a division. On the division, exactly one-half of the members present voted against sending the Dutch proposals to the Committee of Both Kingdoms. Fortunately for the war party, the Speaker, William Lenthall, cast a deciding vote in their favor.[36]

The Covenanters contributed toward this narrow victory by letting it be known, in advance, that they strongly opposed the creation of a separate body. Since only the original committee effectively represented Scottish views on the matter of peace, those who sought to circumvent the Committee of Both Kingdoms obviously wished to deny the Scots their basic rights under the Covenant and treaty and were therefore enemies of Scotland.[37]

Notwithstanding these sharp reminders, sixty-four members of the Commons—a number which included some neutrals—did not want the militants to control negotiations with the king, and they voted as they did even at the risk of alienating the Scots. Many of these same neutral members had appeared quite willing in February and again in May to grant the "violent spirits" control over the direction of the war, which was standard middle-group practice. But apparently others, some of whom previously followed Pym's lead in switching sides on matters of peace and war, now joined the militants on a more consistent basis. Their regular support on all issues enabled the war party to carry out their program in the spring of 1644. The fact that the war party held the initiative in Parliament at this time is another indication that the old middle party no longer operated as a block in English politics.

The split among the moderates on the issue of peace proved to be no accident, for a fortnight later, during a similar division, the same thing occurred. In the intervening period the Lords had come to realize that no peace at all would be forthcoming if they persisted in calling for a new committee. Consequently, on April 13 they offered to turn the making of a treaty over to the Committee of Both Kingdoms, on the condition that it return the propositions within a week's time. Even this minor qualification seemed excessive to the war party, with the result that the Commons divided on the question. Once more the militants secured a victory, but again their margin turned out to be uncomfortably small. They carried, but by only two voices out of 112 votes cast.[38] Nevertheless, the Commons did ultimately agree to a vague time limit being set for the presentation of peace proposals, but the deadline had to be extended several times.[39]

Although they triumphed by the narrowest of margins, the war party had in fact won a significant victory. They themselves did not really desire a treaty at this time; now they could ensure that Parliament's offering would be such that Charles would reject it. The war-party leaders knew that the best way to frame proposals sure to be turned down was to give the Scots a free hand in devising the terms. Thus, while the Committee of Both Kingdoms assumed the responsibility for the treaty, the Scots played the dominant role in its formulation. And among the Scots, Lord Warriston, the most fanatic of them all, the man who distrusted Charles the most, took the lead. Unquestionably Warriston received advice from others, most likely from St. John and Vane, but he remained the guiding spirit. "The Committee of Both Kingdoms," wrote Baillie, "has unanimously agreed to the articles which my Lord Warriston, for the most part, drew up." And in another letter he added: "We have gotten such articles past the Committee of Both Kingdoms and transmitted to both houses as Warriston has brought down; they are of our framing." [40]

Even after both houses studied Warriston's draft, little was done to alter the terms. Those minor changes that Parliament made did not affect the tone of the treaty at all.[41] Nor, when their turn came to evaluate the propositions, did the Scottish Parliament make a single serious modification in the text. The most substantial addition called for by the Estates was that "throughout the whole propositions where it is said Convention of Estates, (Parliament) must be prefixed." [42] In August 1644 the Scottish Estates returned the propositions to London in much the same form as they had been received, and shortly thereafter Parliament gave the stamp of approval to the treaty. The Scots were naturally very pleased with their handiwork. As Baillie happily reported, "The House of Commons on Saturday has passed all the propositions of peace as they came from our Parliament, without the least alteration." [43]

The speed with which the proposed treaty passed from London to Edinburgh and back belied the fact that the terms of this document were actually quite severe. For as they appeared in August, the propositions called for the abolition of episcopacy and requested that the king take the Covenant. Charles would be compelled to commit himself in advance to accept the Westminster Assembly's church settlement, whatever form that should take. The treaty also asked the king to repudiate his cease-fire agreement with the Irish, and to resume war against the rebels in Ireland. Moreover, Parliament would henceforth exercise virtual control over royal ministers. The question of the militia would soon be settled by Parliament, and Charles was to accept their good faith in this matter.[44]

All save the most politically naïve realized that Charles would never accept these terms. Sir Simonds Dewes wrote in his diary that "these propositions were so extreme as I saw not how the King could possibly yield to them." [45] The Venetian ambassador reached very much the same conclusion. "The sole object of the peace proposal," he wrote

> is to deceive the people and to obliterate the opinion which has become universal, that Parliament abhors any treaty. To this end even

> the most strongly opposed have assisted in it, feeling confident from its outrageousness that the King will not listen to it.[46]

Alone, the Scots believed that a possibility of success existed. In a set of orders to Scottish commissioners leaving for London in June 1644, the Estates instructed them

> to conclude with the King if he shall agree unto those propositions as they shall be presented or make only verbal or circumstantial differences in his censures, and which are in no ways prejudicial to the cause or the interests of the Kingdoms.[47]

The disappointment expressed by the Scottish commissioners at Uxbridge in February 1645 can only be explained by the fact that they truly expected Charles to agree to a substantial portion of the terms. Only once in his letters did Baillie seem to realize how little hope existed for the treaty, but even here he was merely reflecting the views of the war-party leaders.[48]

With the task of framing unworkable proposals securely placed in the care of the Scottish commissioners, the war party could direct itself to the sphere of military operations. It will be recalled that one of the main reasons why an ordinance establishing a Committee of Both Kingdoms had been pushed forward so strenuously was the desire on the part of the militants to remove the Lord General from control of the war. Many of Essex's associates regarded the creation of the committee as an affront to him personally, and fought it specifically on these grounds. Whitelock, for example, felt that the Lords wished to alter the membership of the committee in May of 1644 simply

> because divers of that Committee, especially of the Commons, were apprehended not to be so much the General's friends as others who were desired to be brought in.[49]

However, not all of Essex's supporters opposed the Committee of Both Kingdoms. A goodly number of M.P.s, including some former allies of his, voted for the ordinance in February and again in May because they regarded the measure as essential to the effective conduct of the war.[50] Yet all of

Essex's allies, whatever their stripe, maintained a close watch on the committee because they realized that some of its members would not be terribly sorry to see the Lord General's army suffer humiliation.[51]

The Earl of Essex's original distrust of the Committee of Both Kingdoms seemed borne out when it appeared that the committee neglected his army. On several occasions he felt called upon to protest

> against the long delay of the recruiting my army and ill payment (which) have brought me to, that I am grown the pity of my friends and contempt of my enemies, having as yet no forces to take the field with.[52]

And to compound his grievances, the committee began to show (or so Essex thought) a distinct partiality to his rival, Sir William Waller. Making matters still worse for him was the growing number of accounts concerning his alleged treasonable proclivities. Rumors to this effect had been heard for years, but now they began increasing in intensity.[53] All these factors combined to create in Essex's mind a suspicion that persons of influence within the Commons sought his destruction.

Yet when in April Parliament finally provided his army with supplies, Essex in turn showed a great disinclination to begin his campaign. Among other things, he feared that the war party might take advantage of his absence to plan his dismissal. The Venetian ambassador, observing Essex's delaying tactics and their repercussions, wrote:

> Amid the ever growing dangerous dissensions between the two houses, General Essex appears as a fomentor of the differences and also shows his reluctance to obey the command to take the field, in order not to allow his partisans to relax in his interests, or give his opponents or rivals a chance of winning their independence at the expense of his authority, as they pretend.[54]

Nevertheless, an army had to take the field eventually, and even the Lord General realized that he must depart from London sooner or later. That day arrived on May 14 when he at last took his leave of Parliament.

Under the best of circumstances, the Earl of Essex fell far short of the top rank among contemporary military leaders. In May 1644 he went off to war under conditions that were highly unpromising, and with his mind filled with all kinds of doubts and suspicions. His loyalty had been questioned; he must therefore prove himself once again. The body directing the war, the Committee of Both Kingdoms, consisted mainly of his enemies. Consequently, he had to be constantly on his guard against any attempt on their part to misdirect him or to give special treatment to other generals, whom he regarded as his subordinates. In short, Essex did not begin his campaign in the best possible frame of mind, one that would permit him to make rational decisions as to strategy and procedure. The result might have been predicted. He stubbornly refused to obey directives from the Committee of Both Kingdoms, which led to his marching to the west country of England and ultimately to the disastrous defeat he had long sought to avoid: the surrender of his army at Lostwithiel on September 2.[55]

Essex himself avoided the humiliation of negotiating the surrender by escaping from Lostwithiel by sea on the previous day, leaving his men under the second in command, Sir Philip Skippon; and the latter assumed the unpleasant duty of seeking the most favorable terms possible. The Royalists, however, were forced to be generous. Themselves undersupplied with provisions, they could not take prisoners of war, and had to be content with the arms and supplies of their enemy as the reward for their conquest. The Parliamentary army was therefore allowed to return, albeit in humiliating fashion, to its own lines.[56]

Without significant loss of life on either side the king had won a major victory. Lostwithiel provided encouragement to the Royalists, whose fortunes in the war had been declining. And if nothing else, it restored the morale of his forces at a time when the cause seemed in desperate straits. The success in Cornwall helped to nullify the Royalist defeat at Marston Moor exactly two months earlier. It certainly improved their position in southwest England. But even more important, this triumph would strengthen Charles's hand at any future peace table, making him considerably less willing to accept reduction in his sovereignty.

For the Earl of Essex, the whole episode proved ruinous to his military career. By his own doing, he had suffered "a huge loss both of strength and reputation";[57] and he never again regained the prestige he once held. His open disobedience of orders, and the resulting surrender of a major Parliamentary army, played directly into the hands of the militants. Sir Arthur Haselrig received the news of Essex's defeat by bursting into laughter.[58] Even moderate opinion tended to be dismayed at Essex's affront to his civilian superiors, and the subsequent tragic result of his actions. The Presbyterian minister Charles Herle expressed the view that the defeat at Lostwithiel occurred because "the Lord General's army have not spoken right of the Assembly, and that the army hath been privileged to think that this war is only defensive."[59] These were strong words. Yet Herle, usually quite restrained, now accepted the interpretation which had long been circulated by Essex's detractors. Undoubtedly other moderates must have reacted to recent events in a similar fashion.

The declining prestige of the Lord General naturally served to bolster the war party and to vindicate many of their policies as well. It certainly seemed to prove the wisdom of their persistent quest to give control of the war to the Committee of Both Kingdoms. Their wooing of the Scots in order to strengthen Parliament's military position, one year previously, looked even wiser in retrospect. One might expect, therefore, that this period would mark the high point in their relationship with the Covenanters. Oddly enough, however, the opposite proved to be the case. For at this moment, in the late summer of 1644, the alliance had less than a few weeks of life remaining, as Vane and St. John prepared for the inevitable severance, which they now considered essential to their policies.

To understand this reversal of affections on the part of the militants, we must go back to the winter of 1644, when the Scottish army had just entered English territory. At that time the war party felt as optimistic as the Scots in foreseeing immediate successes accruing to the Covenanting army. The Scots, supremely confident, assumed that they would alter Parliament's fortunes almost overnight. But as the months dragged on with no outstanding victories forthcoming, it became evident that the Scots contributed very little to the Parliamentary cause. The lack of any dramatic success was symbolized by the drawn-out siege of the most important royal fortress in the north, the city of Newcastle. As early as February 3, 1644 the Scots summoned Newcastle to surrender. On October 19, eight and one-half months later, Newcastle finally yielded to a Scottish army.[60]

It was perhaps unfortunate for the Covenanters that so very much had been expected from them, because in reality they did have a vital military role to perform: to prevent the coalescing of the northern Royalist army with their southern segment led by Rupert. In addition, they would be expected to clear the north of the king's troops and garrisons. Several contemporaries appreciated their function. Thomas Hobbes wrote in his *Behemoth:*

> In the end of this year [1643] they [Parliament] solicited also the Scots to enter England with an army to suppress the power of the Earl of Newcastle in the north; which was a plain confession that the Parliament's forces were at this time inferior to the King's, and most men thought that if the Earl of Newcastle had then marched southward, and joined his forces with the King's, that most of the Members of Parliament would have fled out of England.[61]

Whitacre made a similar observation when he wrote in his diary on October 13, 1643:

> This day an order was brought into the house by Mr. Solicitor and passed for securing such moneys upon the public faith, as should be sent for the bringing in of 21,000 Scots *which should assist us in the northern parts.*[62]

In this vital task of neutralizing and eventually eliminating the Duke of Newcastle's army, the Scots, however tardily, did produce concrete results. And although these results materialized at a slower pace than the war party had hoped, the very presence of Scottish troops in the north played an important part in Parliament's final victory in the Civil War. The prospect of a Scottish army in control of the north, threatening his northern flank, forced Prince Rupert to take on the combined Anglo-Scottish army at Marston Moor. His disastrous defeat there led inevitably to Parliament's capture of York, and of Newcastle as well. With the north secure, Parliament was then able to plan its operations wholly in the midlands and the southwest. It will be recalled in this connection that the National Army of 1645-1646, the New Model, which brought final victory, devoted its energies exclusively to these regions.

Yet essential though the Scottish contribution may have been, their achievements continued to appear insignificant. They had not brought about that instantaneous end of the war which the more sanguine had predicted, and the inevitable disappointment set in early. Within a few months of their invasion of England a chorus of doubting voices began to be heard in the land, deprecating the Scottish role. As early as March 1644 the Venetian ambassador pointed out how "the hopes of Parliament [have] grown dim that the sword of the Scots would intimidate the King's, and that in consequence the strongest towns would fall into their hands." [63] During the following month the Scottish commissioners in London felt called upon to alert the Earl of Leven about the "jealousies" directed against their army. "Some persons here," they reported,

> have taken occasion to express their thoughts that your forces have not been everyway so active against the enemy's as they in their own expectation had promised to themselves, which misrepresentation of your affairs wants not its own effects.[64]

And Robert Baillie repeatedly reminded his countrymen of the possible ill consequences if they failed to defeat the Royalists. By mid-April he confessed, "We are exceedingly sad and ashamed that our army, so much talked of, has done as yet nothing at all." [65]

Finally, on July 2, 1644, Leven's army joined in bringing about the splendid and dramatic victory against Rupert at Marston Moor. This was the major triumph the Scots in London had longed for; now it had arrived. "Our army," recorded Baillie in his first joyful account of the battle, "fought Prince Rupert, has overthrown his force, taken his cannon and baggage, killed many of his chief officers and chased the rest from York." [66] But poor Baillie's celebration proved somewhat premature. Instead of his brethren receiving the laurels which he felt they deserved, the victory was attributed to the efforts of Oliver Cromwell. Major Harrison, one of Cromwell's closest associates, hastened to London with a version of the battle which singled out Cromwell for special praise. According to

Harrison's account, the Ironsides inflicted the crushing blow on the Cavaliers, thus making Cromwell the hero of the day. To the neutrals this may have sounded like an exaggeration, but when more dispassionate reports began arriving from the North it appeared conclusive that General Cromwell had played the leading part in the victory.[67] July 2, the date of the Battle of Marston Moor, marks the moment when Cromwell began to play an ever greater role in Parliamentary affairs.

Parliament's great triumph over Rupert represents a turning point in the Civil War in several ways. As Denzil Holles later observed, "That day's work at Marston Moor turned the scales, and raised again the fortune of the Parliament, which till that day had very much declined."[68] Militarily, the smashing defeat of the king's army meant that the Royalists would be forced to give up the north. York surrendered shortly afterward, and the city of Newcastle could not possibly hold out for long. Indeed, the length of time it took the Scots to capture the city was little short of a national disgrace.[69]

After Marston Moor the need for a Scottish army diminished. They had performed their main function in the north (although a good many persons in Parliament would not even grant them this credit) and for the remainder of the first Civil War the Scottish army would be involved only in minor sieges whose outcomes were more or less a certainty. The Covenanting army would be merely an appendage of the main body of Parliament's force, the important conflicts taking place in the counties of England far removed from Scottish soldiers. Richard Baxter, the minister, described their role after July 1644 in a manner that reflected English opinion. "After this [Marston Moor]," he observed, "the Scots army lay still in the north a long time, and did nothing till thereby they became odious as a burden to the land."[70]

Another development which added to the lowering of Scottish military prestige, and eventually damaged their effectiveness, was the phenomenal success of the *bête noire* of the Argyll party in Scotland, James Graham, the Earl of Montrose. Just three months after the Scottish troops crossed the Tweed going south, the news reached London that Montrose had gone in the opposite direction in order to harass their rear.[71] By September 1, 1644, he had won a spectacular victory at Tippermuir, and occupied the town of

Perth. During the following winter Montrose caused the Covenanters an even greater amount of concern and embarrassment. But already in the autumn of 1644, his triumphs "diminished our reputation already being joined with the length of the siege at Newcastle," lamented a discouraged Baillie.[72]

The declining importance of Scotland in the struggle with the king forced the war party to reevaluate the Scots' ability to contribute to their main goal: winning the war as soon as possible. From the spring of 1643, when they first revealed their distrust of Essex, the militants had been trying to get together an army which could be counted on to bring victory. Their attempt to make Sir William Waller independent of the Lord General in the summer of 1643 proved abortive. Moreover, events revealed that even Waller lacked the strength of character and the skill necessary to provide the dynamics of victory. Their failure to circumvent Essex's authority led the "violents" to place all their hopes on their northern brethren, for at least the Covenanters had generals and troops who could be trusted. The leaders of the war party therefore did their utmost to encourage the Scottish army. But as the inactivity of the Scots became more evident, the war party again began searching for an army or a reliable general who could defeat the Royalists.

Marston Moor served to bring Oliver Cromwell forward as Parliament's outstanding commander; so that it was only natural for the war party to turn to him, the man responsible for the Roundheads' greatest success to date. Cromwell was tailor-made for the needs of the "violents" and, what is more, his views coincided with theirs: he was a devout Puritan and a militant in politics. Furthermore, there could be no doubt that, as an officer, Cromwell wished to see the war pushed on as long as necessary. As a lieutenant general to the Earl of Manchester in the army of the Eastern Association, he stood in a position to influence the policies of that substantial force. Finally, Cromwell had already demonstrated an ability as a military leader that made him a rare phenomenon among Civil War generals.[73]

There existed, however, one serious problem concerning the war party's adoption of Cromwell as their champion: he and a great many of his troops were either Independents, Brownists, or members of various sects. No concealment of these affiliations was possible, for the Scots knew about the religious character of the Eastern Association's army. Certainly they were aware of Cromwell's affiliations; "the great Independent," Baillie had called him the previous April.[74] To further complicate the situation, the Scots, in the summer of 1644, began to grow restive under the restrictions of the religious truce. For against the spirit of this agreement they gave encouragement to Thomas Edwards, one of the most bigoted and intolerant of English Presbyterians, to print his first savage attack on toleration, *Antapologia.*[75] To men of Edwards's mentality, anyone who was not a rigid Presbyterian must be an enemy. All other religious beliefs, no matter how responsible, would lead the way to anarchy and destruction. The *Apologetical Narration* he referred to as "a good back door to go out at from Brownism to Anabaptism and from Anabaptism to Sebaptism, and from thence to Familisme and Socianisme."[76]

The job of reconciling the increasingly intolerant Scots with an openly Independent Cromwell even temporarily would require an extraordinary amount of discretion, yet this is exactly what Sir Henry Vane, Jr., and Oliver St. John possessed in the summer of 1644. Baillie who, as we know, represented Scottish opinion, demonstrated in his letters how the war party adopted Cromwell as a standard bearer, and how the Scots briefly compromised his views in order to hold on to him. On July 16, just a fortnight after Marston Moor, Baillie wrote about Cromwell's contribution to the victory, and then added:

> The Independents have done so brave service, yea they [are] so strong and considerable a party, that they must not only be tolerated, but in nothing grieved, and no ways to be provoked.

On August 10 he referred again to the indispensability of the Independent soldiers: "For the time they [Parliament] are loath to cast them off, and to put their party to a despair, lest they desert them."[77] It is inconceivable that the Scots could have reached these conclusions (i.e., the need to tolerate the Independents for military purposes) without encouragement from their friends Vane and St. John.

Cromwell's importance as a military leader in 1644 depended almost entirely on his relationship with his commander, the Earl of Manchester. Despite his earlier notoriety as an incendiary (he was the noble appendage to "the Five Members"), Manchester was a weak and indecisive individual, and as is characteristic of such persons, he had delegated a great deal of authority to his subordinate. "He permitted," Baillie observed, "his Lt. General Cromwell to guide all the army at his pleasure." [78] In addition to being much more forceful than his commander, Cromwell, at this stage of the war, was a man who knew what he wanted. He encouraged religious extremists–Independents, Brownists, Socians, etc.–to fight under him, and they, as it turned out, became the most dedicated soldiers produced on either side during the Civil War. Flanking Cromwell as his junior officers were men like Ireton, Harrison, Fleetwood, and Pickering, all devout Puritans as well as first-rate military men.

Cromwell appeared content to continue his association with Manchester indefinitely, for with a few more major triumphs like Marston Moor the war would be over. But after that important battle a sudden change came over Manchester. His whole behavior, as well as his attitudes, underwent a conversion. He sought Cromwell's advice on fewer occasions, with the result that the latter's influence noticeably diminished. More seriously, Manchester evidently lost heart in the war.[79]

This strange transformation in Manchester has been attributed by many historians to a sinister event that preceded Marston Moor. According to this account, while the combined Parliamentary armies of Manchester and Fairfax, and Scottish forces under the Earl of Leven, besieged York in early June, Sir Henry Vane, Jr., representing the Committee of Both Kingdoms, came to discuss military matters. But this apparently routine mission has been interpreted as part of an unsavory scheme. Vane, it is claimed, proposed to the three generals that Charles I be deposed, and that he be succeeded by another.[80] Allegedly nothing came of this proposal, since the generals rejected it out of hand; and obviously Charles remained king for another four and one-half years. Yet the very suggestion of such a revolutionary action by Vane is said to have had a sobering effect upon all three officers, especially on Manchester. This minor event, we are told, assumed vital importance in the future, for Manchester became alarmed when he learned that his own aide, Oliver Cromwell, showed sympathy for the proposal. According to Gardiner:

> since the day on which Vane, backed doubtless by Cromwell, had advocated the actual or virtual dethronement of the King, the General of the Army of the Association regarded his Lieutenant-General with grave suspicion.[81]

This account of Vane's mission does not survive close scrutiny of the avilable evidence. Largely based on hearsay and rumor, the story of a plot to depose Charles I remains, at best, an unproven hypothesis. An analysis of this hypothesis [82] forces us to conclude that Sir Henry Vane, Jr., went north in June 1644 for the reasons specified in his instructions, which concerned matters of a military nature. To those who contend that Vane stood too high in government circles to be sent on such a routine mission, it should be pointed out that since one of the three generals to be consulted was a Scot, Vane was the best equipped to deal with all of them together. On the very same day that Vane received orders to go to York, John Crew, another reputable member of the Committee of Both Kingdoms, went on a similar mission to Essex's army.[83]

The answer to the related question of why Manchester lost interest in the war at this juncture is far less obscure than many historians have suggested. Edward Montague, the Earl of Manchester, was a mild-mannered individual, "a sweet, meek man," as Baillie described him.[84] Never a dynamic leader, he certainly did not possess the force of character essential during a time of upheaval like the English Revolution. His generalship, even in its better moments, lacked vigor. Such was the case before Marston Moor. As the Venetian ambassador once observed:

> The Earl of Manchester has advanced to Selby and has orders to join them [the Scots army], but whether from reluctance to go far from the Associated Counties or for lack of courage, he has always shown himself very slow in carrying out his orders.[85]

Characteristically, Manchester took a middle position in politics. He had assumed command of the army of the Eastern Association with the hope that Charles would eventually become reasonable enough to sue for terms with Parliament. But the crushing defeat inflicted on the Royalists in Yorkshire pointed to the strong likelihood that the king would be beaten too decisively for a conditional peace. This possibility grew into a probability when the general's own lieutenant continued to make rash statements concerning the future settlement. It undoubtedly crossed Manchester's mind that if militants like Cromwell prescribed the terms of peace, then the government and social order for which he was fighting would be transformed beyond all recognition.[86]

It would seem that the growing radicalization of the conflict, rather than any one single event, played a major role in changing Manchester's attitude toward the war. By avoiding battle and resisting all efforts to defeat the king's forces conclusively, he hoped to prolong the struggle, thereby putting off the day when Parliament would dictate the peace. An inconclusive outcome on the battlefield might very well compel Parliament to accept moderate terms for a settlement.

Following the surrender of York on July 16, 1644 Manchester delayed for ten days at Doncaster, and then procrastinated three whole weeks at Lincoln. He refused to grant Colonel Lilburne permission to summon Tickhill Castle, and when Lilburne took it upon himself to seize the fortress (without encountering any difficulty), Manchester threatened to have him hanged for disobeying orders. During the next weeks the Earl turned a deaf ear to the pleas of his subordinates to surround the Royalist stronghold at Newark. And when on August 8 the Committee of Both Kingdoms called upon him to pursue Rupert into Chester, he declined the order on the grounds that his army had suffered too many "indispositions and infections."[87]

In all fairness to him, the number of his troops had undoubtedly been reduced by the extended campaign of the past months, but this defect was partially remedied when the committee requested the Eastern Association to supply him with 1,800 more soldiers.[88] While the letters urging him to engage his troops continued to arrive from London, Manchester remained immobile at Lincoln. On September 4 he at last decided that the time had come to depart from his resting spot; but after receiving the news of Essex's defeat in Cornwall he drew up his troops at Huntington, where he intended to stay indefinitely. When some of his officers recommended that he march the army westward, Manchester allegedly replied that he would hang anyone who repeated such advice.[89]

Unfortunately for the earl, his subordinate, Oliver Cromwell, refused to sit by patiently while his commander weakened Parliament's chances in the Civil War. Realizing that he could no longer influence him, Cromwell decided to make a public issue out of Manchester's behavior. There is good reason to believe that he consulted with Vane and St. John before acting, and that they tempered his desire to smash out at the earl.[90] Although the responsibility for the Eastern Association army's failure to fight rested solely with their military leader, Cromwell and his advisers chose not to take on a man of Manchester's stature just yet. Instead, they focused their attack on the Scottish Presbyterian officer, Major General Crawford, who recently had become Manchester's confidant. A charge was duly made against General Crawford blaming him for the inactivity of the army, and demanding that he be removed from his position. Unless action was taken at once, Cromwell and all his colonels would resign their commissions.[91]

By September 7, 1644 the news of the dispute reached London, causing a great deal of agitation there. The Scots firmly believed that Cromwell and his Independent colleagues precipitated the controversy, and they quickly sided with their own countryman, Crawford, whom they regarded as innocent. Despite their predisposition, however, the Covenanters did not wish to see Parliament's military position suffer because of internecine quarrels, and they therefore pressed for a solution that would bring about a reconciliation.[92] The constructive approach pursued by the Scots found support within the Committee of Both Kingdoms, which immediately sent a message to Manchester recommending that he have "all personal differences so composed and forgotten as shall enable them [the officers] to prosecute the war effectively to a happy and speedy end."[93]

Their warning to avoid disunity at all costs took on additional meaning when the report of Essex's surrender at Lostwithiel reached London on September 10. The committee responded to the disaster by sending off duplicate letters to several officers, including Manchester and Cromwell, begging them "to lay aside all disputes" for the moment.[94] Officially, then, the members of the committee assumed a neutral position between the claims of Cromwell and the conduct of Manchester, but unofficially their sympathies lay with Cromwell. On the day before the conciliatory letter was issued, John Crew penned a personal word of advice to the Earl of Manchester in which he called upon the earl to strive for unity among his officers, and he added: "I beseech your Lordship (although I need not do it) to give all respect to L. G. Cromwell."[95]

Manchester, regarding the matter one of principle, chose not to accept Crew's suggestion. But with no solution to the threatened revolt of his junior officers, he decided to make a personal appearance in London for the purpose of strengthening his case. Once there, however, he soon realized his miscalculation, for in Parliament Cromwell's supporters had prepared the ground for their hero. On September 13, when the lieutenant general, fast on Manchester's heels, appeared in London for the first time since Marston Moor, the House of Commons moved their

> thanks to Lieutenant General Cromwell for his fidelity in the cause in hand; and in particular for the faithful service performed by him in the late battle near York, where God made him a special instrument in obtaining that great victory.[96]

It represented a great distinction for him to be so honored, for the Commons did not often extend such congratulations to military men. Parliament had last acted in this manner when the Earl of Essex received congratulations for his relief of Gloucester, a year before.[97] Since Cromwell was singled out for honor, while no mention had been made of Manchester's contribution, the earl must have realized that Parliamentary opinion strongly opposed him. When he saw as well that he had no backing from the Committee of Both Kingdoms, he wisely capitulated.

A compromise solution to the controversy, offered by the committee, finally met with Manchester's grudging approval. Cromwell agreed to withdraw his charges against General Crawford in return for Manchester's promise to pursue the war vigorously in the west of England. The earl would join forces with Sir William Waller in the coming campaign, and to ensure that disputes among the officers were kept under control, two members of the Committee of Both Kingdoms would henceforth accompany the troops in the field. Once agreed upon, these terms were issued by the committee on September 21.[98] Superficially a rather simple arrangement, the settlement carried two significant admissions. By readily agreeing to drop the charges against Crawford in return for a promise from Manchester, Cromwell admitted that the blame for the army's inactivity rested not with the adviser but with the commander himself; while Manchester's acceding to a plan to prosecute the war carried the suggestion that he had in fact been inactive previously. The implications of these two inconspicuous confessions would be drawn in the future, for if the army of the Eastern Association failed to move, the responsibility would rest with one man alone.

Apparently the Scottish commissioners played a key role in bringing about the reconciliation. With the war far from over, and Montrose a growing threat in their homeland, they feared that disunity in Parliament's ranks would strengthen the Royalists and ultimately work to their own disadvantage. From the beginning the Scots had always favored measures for improving Parliament's military position. Consequently, in the dispute between Crawford and Cromwell they volunteered their services as a disinterested outside party who could settle disagreements so that the armies might again take the field. The commissioners themselves described their task thus:

> We conceive it our duty to apply ourselves for reconciling those differences, and to contribute our best endeavors for their [the generals'] union.[99]

The Scotsman who had done, as Baillie put it, "a good deal of noble service" to settle the dispute was the newly arrived chancellor of Scotland, the Earl of Loudoun. A member of the Clan Campbell, Loudoun represented the Argyll faction in politics. Always considered one of the best diplomats in Scotland, he had attended the king during the Oxford negotiations in the spring of 1643, and he would participate, in one capacity or another, in all subsequent Scottish negotiations with Charles.[100]

Loudoun had come to England in mid-September for the purpose of adding new vigor to the Scottish delegation there. The decision by the Scots to send such an important personage was taken after the occurrence of two events which threatened to reduce the importance of Scotland as a partner in the war. The first, Parliament's dramatic victory at Marston Moor, meant for all intents that now the north would be easily pacified, thus diminishing the need for a Scottish army. Montrose's surprising and humiliating defeat of the Covenanting forces at Tippermuir was the second. A Scottish contemporary summed up the reason for Loudoun's mission in the following fashion:

> That the King was thought to be brought so low, that the Parliament of England began to believe themselves able to prosecute the work without the assistance of the Scots, and that therefore they began to undervalue them, and so wish to be rid of them; so that the Parliament of Scotland, having considered that if the Parliament of England should hear the worst of Montrose's late victory, it would foment that unbrotherly humor in them, they therefore held it necessary that the Lord Chancellor should go up to put a good face on things.[101]

The Earl of Loudoun could not have chosen a more inauspicious time to come to England. He arrived at the moment when the Scottish alliance with the war party had dissolved, and the Covenanters, for the first time, found themselves alone on the English political stage.

During the summer of 1644 a noticeable change had taken place in the religious policy of the war party: they became more openly committed to toleration for the purpose of winning over the Independent element in the army. At approximately the same time the Covenanters had become more rigid than before in their desire to stamp out the sects. The Scottish ministers, never really enamored of the religious truce, now openly demonstrated their contempt for the idea of toleration. They found it increasingly tedious to participate in the lengthy debates of the Westminster Assembly for the purpose of proving the Presbyterian system to be according to the word of God, a fact that they regarded as self-evident. For tactical reasons they had gone along with the English divines, but they had done so with the expectation that Presbyterianism would be enacted within a reasonable time. They would listen to "erroneous opinions" only so long as the desired church settlement showed signs of being established. But unfortunately for the Scots, the assembly never moved as quickly as they hoped, and agreement on various sections of the church government took forever to be reached. Moreover, whenever the assembly did finally agree to any item it would be sent on to Parliament, where months often passed before anything further would be heard of the matter. For example, in April 1644 Parliament received the assembly's Directory for Ordination and the twelve Doctrinal Propositions on Ordination, yet a half year went by before a *revised* ordinance for ordination of ministers became law.[102]

By August the Scots had become quite restive over the delay in settling religion. In the middle of the month the commissioners from the kirk, in a note to Parliament, called attention to their long, patient, but futile attendance at the Westminster Assembly.

> All this time nothing hath issued forth from the advice of the Reverend Assembly here, and the authority of the Honorable Houses of Parliament for settling uniformity in divine worship and church government.

They concluded their paper by urging the "expediting of this great work."[103]

Yet on the very same day that the kirk commissioners showed their displeasure with the "neglect of religion," the Commons returned the ordinance for ordination to the assembly with amendments appended. The most crucial of these, the statement that the measure was to be provisional only, meant that the church discipline could not be fixed for all times.[104] The Scottish divines took immediate offense at this ruling and decided to make a stand on principle. Joined by sympathetic English Presbyterians, they persuaded the assembly to ignore the statement of the Commons. In a defiant manner they returned the ordinance to Parliament in exactly the same form in which it had appeared when first sent off in April. But Parliament had no stomach for claims of *jure divino.* The final ordinance read: "It was resolved, upon the question, that the intention of the House was and is that the rule of ordination should be only *pro tempore.*" And with this reservation the measure became law on October 4.[105]

Parliament's strong opposition to an overpowerful Presbyterian ministry, latent for a long time, was now openly stated for the Covenanters to see. Equally clear to them should have been the growing evidence of the war party's sympathy for religious toleration. Nevertheless, the Scots continued to act under the assumption that enough pressure from Scotland, backed by Scottish military successes, would compel both Houses to accept a Presbyterian church government. They gave no sign that they perceived the warnings signaling the imminent demise of their alliance with the militants.[106]

The dissolution of the partnership between Scots and war party coincided with Cromwell's return to Parliament on September 13; ironically, the Scots themselves had set the stage beforehand. Just a few days prior to Cromwell's arrival in London, the Assembly of Divines, after conspicuous Scottish prodding, urged Parliament to suppress Anabaptists and Antinomians. Before the advice had been sent, the Independents in the assembly insisted that they had the right to demur from the majority opinion, and they sought to present their position before Parliament.[107] The dissenting views of the Independents, expressed on this occasion, reveal a change in their position on toleration. In their *Apologetical Narration,* published eight months earlier, they had very carefully restricted freedom of religion to responsible religious groups like themselves. Now, under the pressure of events, and especially because they desired to gain the support of the religious "non-conformists" in the army, the Independents came out for the toleration of Anabaptists and Antinomians.

On September 13, the day Cromwell appeared in the Commons to receive its acclaim for his military service, the house was in the midst of a debate concerning religion. During the heated discussion, Oliver St. John unexpectedly arose to recommend that the Committee of Both Kingdoms and the assembly

> do take into consideration the differences in opinion of the members of the Assembly in point of church government, and to endeavor a

> union if it be possible, and in case that cannot be done, to endeavor the finding out some ways how tender consciences, who cannot in all things submit to the common rule which shall be established, may be borne with.[108]

Thus for the first time St. John, one of the most influential members of Parliament, publicly stated his preference for religious freedom. In addition, he favored giving the Independents an equal voice in the assembly, one that would be out of proportion to their numbers. Since Parliament had just received the divines' request for suppression of Antinomians and Anabaptists, St. John's plea for toleration must be taken as referring not only to Independents, but to the sects as well. His motion, backed by Vane, Haselrig, and of course by Cromwell, passed the house without any marked difficulty. Although St. John introduced the measure the impetus clearly came from Cromwell. Thus Baillie observed that "this day Cromwell has obtained an order of the House of Commons to refer to the Committee of Both Kingdoms the accommodation or toleration of the Independents." [109] The newly formed coalition between Oliver Cromwell and the war party had borne its first fruit.

Until this day the Covenanters, never too perceptive in English political dealings, and gently misguided by Vane and St. John, failed to detect any drastic change in their allies. As a result, St. John's motion, delivered without warning, came as a rude and bitter shock. The blow was all the more stunning as it had been struck by the Scots' most faithful champions. "Our greatest friends, Sir Henry Vane and the Solicitor," moaned a distraught Baillie,

> are the main procurers of all this; and that without any regard to us, who have saved their nation, and brought these two persons to the height of the power now they enjoy, and use to our prejudice.[110]

Baillie might have had an exaggerated view of the Scottish contribution, but he seems to have understood precisely what was taking place in Parliamentary politics: "Sir Henry Vane, our most intimate friend, joining with a new faction to procure liberty for the Sects." [111] Richard Baxter, the

English cleric, saw the situation in much the same way, "But in all this work," he concluded,

> the Vanists in the house and Cromwell in the army, joined together, out-witted and over-reached the rest, and carried on the interest of the Sectaries in special, while they drew the Religious Party along as for the interest of Godliness in the general.[112]

The Commons' recommendation that a committee be established to bring about "an accommodation of tender consciences" received the backing of Stephen Marshall, so that once again we find this influential minister attempting to effect a reconciliation dictated by political necessity. The Scots apparently believed that he had collaborated with St. John in framing the accommodation order,[113] but the evidence to support their charge is conjectural. For while Marshall did his best to see the ordinance effectuated, there is reason to believe that his conversion to the Vane-St. John-Cromwell position came at the last minute. We know that he had long favored a compromise which would enable the various religious groups to devote their energies to winning the war, but only a month previously Marshall openly opposed toleration for the sects. On August 9 he accompanied Dr. Burgess to Parliament with a petition protesting the rapid increase in the number of Anabaptists and Antinomians.[114] Another reason for believing that Marshall had not been a party to the accommodation order was the fact that he had not prepared opinion in the assembly to favor the measure. Previously, whenever he tried to bring together opposing sides, he could be confident of the backing of other moderate Presbyterian ministers. Yet when, in September, he joined the religious Independents in their various maneuvers for obtaining an assurance of toleration, men like Vines, Herle, Palmer, and Temple deserted him and sided with the Covenanters.[115]

The endeavors of the English Presbyterians and their Scottish brethren to obstruct an extensive plan calling for accommodation prevented the religious Independents from registering any outstanding gain. In fact, the Grand Committee set up by the Commons, composed of members of Parliament and ministers, accomplished nothing concrete whatsoever. After five weeks the house voted to dissolve the committee, and the war party did little to prevent its adjournment.[116] Indeed, it is quite likely that the motion to abolish the committee did not meet with any great resistance from Vane and St. John. As far as they were concerned the furor over this episode achieved one important, indirect result: for in the confrontation between Presbyterian and Independent, the assembly's desire to suppress Antinomians and Anabaptists seems to have been forgotten.

Vane and St. John had backed the original order on accommodation largely to demonstrate the unity between their party and Cromwell. Yet the continued existence of the Grand Committee began to cause them a good deal of embarrassment, and it is reasonable to suspect that they welcomed its termination. Their apparent change of heart stemmed mainly from the committee's divisive effect on the militants themselves. Until now the party had remained together because its members agreed on the fundamental issues of war and peace. The question of a religious settlement had been tactfully left in the background.

At this time, in September and October 1644, some of the Presbyterian members of the war party began rejecting the stand taken by their leaders in regard to toleration. This became evident from the first meeting of the special committee. Lords Say and Wharton, along with Sr. Henry Vane, Jr., and Oliver St. John, "proposed immediately from this committee to get toleration of Independency concluded in the House of Commons, long before anything should be gotten so much as reported from the Assembly about Presbyteries." [117] But during the sessions they had to sit quietly while several warlike Presbyterians stood up to denounce their proposals. "Mr. Rous, Mr. Tate and Mr. Prideaux, among the ablest members of the House of Commons, opposed them to their face," observed Baillie. He might have added that these men were among the ablest members of the war party as well. Rather than risk any lasting split in their ranks, Vane and St. John beat a hasty retreat.

The short history of the Grand Committee thus witnessed, among other things, Sir Henry Vane, Jr.'s, backtracking from his original position of full toleration for the sects and complete intransigence to the Presbyterians. The first meeting of the committee had been on September 20; by the 15th of the following month one finds Vane speaking as an Erastian, arguing that Parliament may alter any rule "established by the Assembly."[118] At the last meeting of the committee, just ten days later, Vane became considerably more conciliatory to the Presbyterians, even toning down his language so as not to offend. And while disagreements persisted between the religious Independents and the Presbyterians, the whole atmosphere had altered to the extent that calm discussion was now possible.[119] At this point the committee terminated its sessions with very little to show for its efforts. For the militants it ended none too soon. With the issue of toleration put aside for the moment, and the temporary convulsion within the party healed, the party could once again prepare itself for the coming political struggles.

The one major result of the attempt to accommodate tender consciences was that it brought the alliance between the war party and the Scots to a conclusion. As one of the Scots bitterly recalled a year later:

> The first and main occasion of mistake betwixt those men and the Scots, was the church government. . . . After much struggling, things being brought near a conclusion, some of those upon whose friendship the Scots had till then so much relied, did declare themselves to be altogether adverse to the government the Scots were so desirous of. . . . Ever since that day to this day, those men having withdrawn their temporary affection from the Scots, have opposed their counsels, and crossed their proceedings in every thing wherein they are concerned.[120]

For the Covenanters, the unexpected break with their allies served as a sharp reminder of the vicissitudes of English politics. The betrayal by their supposed friends remained a bitter pill to swallow, and they recovered from the shock only with difficulty. Yet if the Scots wished to see their aims in the Civil War fulfilled, they had to persist in their efforts to influence the English Parliament; and this would entail entering into new alliances in London, in order to make the most of their position. The Covenanters may have been a bit confused by recent events, but they never lost their optimism.

NOTES

1. *Mercurius Aulicus,* March 23, 1645.
2. Buchanan, p. 53.
3. Dewes, 166, fol. 18.
4. Ibid., fols. 47, 53, 101 v.
5. L.J., VI, pp. 464, 512.
6. Whitacre, fol. 278.
7. C.S.P.D., 1644, pp. 25-27, 44, 73.
8. C.J., III, p. 411.
9. Dewes, 166 fol. 19-19v.
10. Ibid.
11. C.J., III, p. 411.
12. Dewes, 166, fol. 36.
13. *Acts and Ordinances,* I, pp. 398-405.
14. Baillie, II, pp. 178, 187; Buchanan, p. 51.
15. Dewes, 166, fol. 58 v.
16. Ibid., fol 61 v-62; C.J., III, p. 483.
17. The Scots were very distressed with the Lords on this occasion. See C.J., III, p. 496.
18. See Dewes, 166, fol. 64, for the active role played by Prideaux, Strode, and Lisle.
19. L.J., VI, p. 550.
20. Whitelock, II, p. 258.
21. Dewes, 166, fol. 64v.
22. C.J., III, p. 502; ibid., p. 391, for the February vote.
23. Ibid., p. 496.
24. Whitacre, f. 278 (italics added).
25. Baillie, II, p. 187.
26. *Acts and Ordinances,* I, pp. 479-480.
27. *Instructions,* Jan. 28, 1644.

28. *Parliament of Scotland,* VI, p. 70.
29. Dewes, 166, fol. 14 v.
30. C.J., III, p. 146.
31. L.J., VI, p. 458.
32. C.J., III, p. 428.
33. L.J., VI, pp. 471, 477.
34. Ibid., p. 479; C.J., III, pp. 435-436.
35. Whitelock, II, pp. 246-248.
36. C.J., III, p. 443.
37. Baillie, II, pp. 154-155.
38. C.J., III, p. 458.
39. L.J., VI, p. 527. It was finally submitted on April 29.
40. Baillie, II, pp. 172, 177.
41. C.J., III, pp. 472, 483-484.
42. *Parliament of Scotland,* VI, pp. 129-130. Parenthesis in the original.
43. Baillie, II, p. 222; C.J., III, pp. 594-596.
44. L.J., VI, pp. 531-534. For a more detailed discussion of the terms of the Uxbridge Treaty, see chap. IV, below.
45. Dewes, 166, fol. 109 v.
46. C.S.P. Ven., p. 146.
47. *Instructions,* June 28, 1644. Of course, the Scots would not accept the king's terms if they differed fundamentally from those of Parliament.
48. Baillie, II, p. 211. In the same letter Baillie wrote that "if we should begin to treat with him [Charles] on the alteration of any of them, it will draw both to a great length and a dangerous losing of our ground." This was a point the war party had been making for a long time.
49. Whitelock, II, p. 257.
50. Dewes, 166, fols. 36, 98 v. Glyn and Earle were two friends of the Lord General who supported the committee.
51. Holles, pp. 24-26; Dewes, 166, fol. 113.
52. L.J., VI, p. 505.
53. C.S.P. Ven., p. 78; L.J., VI, p. 527.
54. C.S.P., Ven., p. 102.
55. *Civil War,* II, p. 18. For a fuller description of Essex's western

campaign, see Vernon Snow, *Essex the Rebel, the Life of Robert Devereaux, the Third Earl of Essex* (Lincoln, Neb., 1970), chap. 17.

56. Ibid., pp. 18-19.
57. Baillie, II, p. 229.
58. Dewes, 166, fol. 113.
59. George Gillespie, *Notes and Debates and Proceedings of the Assembly of Divines* (Edinburgh, 1841), pp. 68-69.
60. *Civil War,* II, p. 44.
61. Thomas Hobbes, *Behemoth,* in F. Maseres, *Select Tracts,* Part II (London, 1815), p. 574.
62. Whitacre, fol. 167 (italics added).
63. C.S.P. Ven., p. 80.
64. H.W. Meikle, ed., *Correspondence of the Scottish Commissioners in London* (London, 1917), p. 19.
65. Baillie, II, p. 166.
66. Ibid., p. 201.
67. Ibid., pp. 208-209.
68. Holles, pp. 17-18.
69. Baillie, II, p. 231.
70. Baxter, p. 49.
71. Yonge, 18, 779, fol. 96.
72. Baillie, II, p. 234.
73. Sir Charles Firth, *Oliver Cromwell* (London, 1900), remains the best biography. But also see Christopher Hill's brilliant interpretation, *God's Englishman* (New York, 1970).
74. Ibid., p. 153.
75. T.T., E. 1 (1), July 13, 1644. See below p. 00, for further evidence of growing Scottish rigidity.
76. Ibid.
77. Baillie, II, pp. 208-209, 218.
78. Ibid., p. 299.
79. *Manchester's Quarrel,* pp. 96-99.
80. Dame Veronica Wedgwood puts forward the idea that Charles Louis was suggested as the likely candidate. See *The King's War* (London, 1958), p. 349.

81. *Civil War,* II, p. 20.
82. See my article, "The 'Plot' to Depose Charles I in 1644," *Bulletin of the Institute of Historical Research,* XLV (1971), pp. 216-223. Professor MacCormack, op. cit., p. 33, n. 51, has attempted to answer my criticism of the traditional view, but except for one rather unclear source (Buchanan), he supplies no new evidence. The other references to the two foreign diplomats, who circulated the rumor, do not add much.
83. C.S.P.D., 1644, pp. 197-198. Vane's mission concerned the securing of the county of Lancashire, and carried the proposal that the siege of York be abandoned for the present. It may also be recalled that at this time Rupert was marching north with his army.
84. Baillie, II, p. 229.
85. C.S.P. Ven., p. 110. This was written on June 4, 1644.
86. Colonel Pickering heard Manchester say on one occasion: "It was easy to begin a war but no man knew when it would end." C.S.P.D., 1644, pp. 151-152.
87. *Manchester's Quarrel,* pp. 80-81; C.S.P.D., 1644, pp. 149, 406, 417.
88. C.S.P.D., 1644, pp. 407-410.
89. Ibid., p. 150.
90. C.J., III, p. 617.
91. W.C. Abbott, *Writings and Speeches of Oliver Cromwell,* vol. I (Cambridge, Mass., 1937), p. 302. *(In his narrative. . . .)*
92. Baillie, II, p. 230.
93. C.S.P.D., 1644, p. 481.
94. Ibid., pp. 491-492.
95. H.M.C., Manchester MSS, p. 61.
96. C.J., III, p. 626.
97. Ibid., p. 255.
98. C.S.P.D., 1644, p. 526.
99. Meikle, pp. 43-45.
100. D.N.B.
101. Henry Guthry, *Memoirs* (Glasgow, 1747), p. 165.
102. C.J., III, p. 466; *Acts and Ordinances,* I, pp. 521-526 (italics added).
103. L.J., VI, pp. 674-675.

104. C.J., III, p. 592; Baillie, II, p. 198.
105. C.J., III, p. 593.
106. A hint of the imminent split came on September 9, when Vane joined Haselrig in opposing the Scots on some religious matters, including the idea of *jure divino.* See Gillespie, pp. 67-68.
107. Baillie, II, p. 236; Gillespie, p. 66.
108. C.J., III, p. 626.
109. Baillie, II, p. 226.
110. Ibid., p. 230.
111. Ibid., p. 231.
112. Baxter, p. 47.
113. Baillie, II, p. 234.
114. C.J., III, p. 584; Dewes, 166, fol. 105 v.
115. Baillie, II, p. 236.
116. Ibid., p. 240.
117. Ibid., p. 237.
118. Gillespie, p. 106.
119. Ibid., p. 107.
120. Buchanan, pp. 54-55.

III

A New Army

When the leaders of the war party unexpectedly began advocating religious toleration, the Covenanters suddenly realized how carefully sheltered they had been from the realities of English political life. Obviously their former allies had found it convenient to present the Scottish commissioners with a one-sided analysis of events, in order to ensure that they followed a militant course. For their part, the Scots had been perfectly content to follow along, having no reason to suspect the source of their ready-made point of view. Despite their lack of experience with English affairs, the association with the militants made them feel secure. As we know, this sense of security had little basis in fact; and in September 1644 the sheltering structure crumbled to pieces.

For the first time since entering the war, the Covenanters had to make their own way in English politics. The alignments in Parliament, which had seemed so logical and clear just a few months before, now became confusing and quite inexplicable. Favors which had come to them easily in the past, when provided by the war party, were no longer forthcoming. As Clarendon acutely observed, the Scots found "neither their army nor themselves so much considered as before, nor any conditions performed towards them with any punctuality." [1] And to a larger extent than before, they began to be criticized regularly in the chambers of Parliament.

At the end of September the Scottish commissioners heard the first of a long series of complaints registered against their army, complaints which would be repeated throughout the remaining two years of the first Civil War. Sir William Armine, writing from the north of England, sent a letter to the Speaker of the Lords, charging the Scottish army with "plundering, spoiling and wasting" the territory they occupied.[2] Armine had been one of the commissioners who went to Edinburgh in August 1643 to help bring the Scots into the war. An active member of the war party, he remained a close associate of another former friend of the Scots, Sir Henry Vane, Jr.

As we saw, Vane, St. John, and other war-party leaders had previously acted as unofficial spokesmen in Parliament on behalf of their allies, to ensure that the Scottish army received its share of supplies. They did not always succeed. But in the months following September the Scots would discover that the meager funds which the militants provided for them in the past seemed generous compared to what they now received. The problems of provisions had become more serious, especially since June, when 10,000 additional Scottish soldiers came into England. By the fall of 1644 approximately 31,000 men shared the allotment of supplies originally intended for 21,000. On October 11 an attempt was made in the Commons to hold the whole country–and not just the northern counties–responsible for the financing of the Covenanters, in order to obtain a more regular supply of money. Yet despite the obvious need, in the division which followed on that day, the Scots suffered a setback. Led on this occasion by two warlike Presbyterians, Edmund Prideaux and Zouch Tate, the lower house voted to keep them completely dependent upon the scant resources of the north.[3]

Deserted by the war party, and still suspicious of the peace group, the Scots chose to remain unallied for the moment. They had always adhered, more or less, to a certain fundamental approach to English affairs, which, for lack of another course of action, could be reverted to for the time being.

This was their "middle-party" position of working for both war and peace at the same time. A set of instructions had been sent to the commissioners from Edinburgh, back in June 1644, which read in part:

> If there fall out any division in England (which God forbid) you shall do your utmost endeavor to prevent and remove them, and if that be impossible you shall countenance the best affected, that are the firmest to the Covenant, treaty [of November 1643], joint declarations and to the interest of both Kingdoms.[4]

In September the Scottish commissioners found to their chagrin that they themselves were party to a division. Consequently, and perhaps wisely, the Covenanters decided to assume once again their role of mediators. We have already seen how they performed this function by bringing about a compromise between Manchester and Cromwell in September. As best they could, the Scots would try throughout the autumn to conciliate various differences arising within Parliament. Thus in a letter written in mid-October to Lord Warriston, then with Waller's army, the Scottish commissioners requested that he

> shall contribute [his] best endeavors to unite the armies and settle a good understanding betwixt the Lord General, my Lord Manchester, and Sir William Waller, amongst themselves and with us in pursuance of the ends expressed in the Covenant and Treaty for settling religion and peace, and preventing all new factions and designs tending to the division of the Kingdoms and their particular prejudices.[5]

The Scots continued to operate without allies in Parliament, pursuing their "middle-party" propensities, through the winter. Spring would find them moving into the camp of the peace party, though this was a gradual process.[6] The man who foresaw the possibilities of a peace group/Scottish alliance, and began working as early as September 1644 to bring it about, was the French resident, the Marquis of Sabran. For reasons of dynastic commitment, the French Crown sought to obtain a settlement in England favorable to Charles I; obviously the restoration of Henrietta Maria, a French queen, would be in the interest of France. Nevertheless, Cardinal Mazarin did not wish to get his country embroiled in an English war at a time when France had more than her share of difficulties on the European continent. Therefore, instead of sending over soldiers and supplies to assist the Royalist cause, he sent the Marquis of Sabran with strict instructions to encourage an immediate and peaceful settlement. Sabran's other objective was to revive friendly relations between France and her traditional ally, Scotland.[7]

An experienced and capable diplomat, Sabran attempted to combine the two aims set out in his instructions. As a means of getting the Scots back across their border, he would convince them that they should adopt a more pacific approach. He sought to persuade them to soften the terms of the forthcoming treaty with Charles. "I frequently meet the Scottish deputies and try to get them to modify certain articles, but they are irreconcilable nevertheless," he wrote to Cardinal Mazarin.[8] The Earl of Loudoun's arrival in London, coinciding as it did with the Scottish disillusionment with the war party, permitted Sabran to be considerably more optimistic. Before long he reported to Mazarin how the Scots truly desired a peaceful settlement with Charles, one that would preserve some of the Crown's original splendor. Nevertheless, Sabran could not help being aware that the stringent articles of peace designed by the Committee of Both Kingdoms, and already approved by both Parliament and the Scottish Estates, stood little hope of being altered.[9]

The French resident, of course, was not alone in realizing that Parliament's proposals in their present form would never win Charles's approval. Through his connection with the Earl of Holland and the Countess of Carlisle, Sabran learned that the leadership of the peace group also feared the consequences of the coming negotiations. They knew that despite the stringency of its terms, Charles's rejection of the treaty would prove a boon to the war party. For no matter how predictable his reaction, the militants could then argue that the king did not want peace. Faced with the problem of achieving a settlement on the basis of these impossible proposals, the peace group finally hit upon a solution to their dilemma. Holles and Stapleton devised a plan whereby Charles would be asked to accept the present treaty in principle, despite the fact that the conditions offered were completely unpalatable to him. Once he had demonstrated his willingness to negotiate, it would be possible, or so the peace party conceived, to modify Parliament's demands. Holles actually intended to present this scheme to the king when the Parliamentary delegation traveled up to Oxford in November.[10]

The Scottish commissioners learned about the peace party's project from the Marquis de Sabran, who now served as an informal courier between the two groups. At this stage, however, the Covenanters were reluctant to become involved, and they chose to pretend that the whole matter did not concern them.[11] Thus, while three Scottish commissioners accompanied the Parliamentary delegation that met with the king, they remained unobtrusive throughout the proceedings.

The delegation arrived in Oxford on November 23, 1644. As might have been predicted beforehand, the reception given to both them and their proposals was curt and cold. Even the most sanguine among the delegates obviously realized that Charles could never agree to terms that, in fact, asked him "to part with his church, his crown and his friends," as he explained. When the commissioners read aloud the treaty to the king and his councillors, several of the provisions were greeted with derisive laughter. In addition to reacting in a most sarcastic fashion to the limits on the powers of the representatives (they could not negotiate), Charles showed utter contempt for the three Scotsmen, whom he regarded as outsiders.[12]

The leaders of the peace group, realizing that the king must be approached with their plan at once, asked some of the royal councillors to arrange a private audience. On that first evening Denzil Holles and Bulstrode Whitelock went to the Earl of Lindsay's residence, and within fifteen minutes of their arrival Charles entered accompanied by his retinue. After the usual courtesies the king suddenly launched into a tirade against the unrealistic character of the terms offered by Parliament. Instead of trying to defend these terms (which he himself found equally unrealistic),

Holles unraveled the peace party's scheme. It was imperative, he reasoned, that the king agree to an immediate conclusion of the war by accepting Parliament's present offer. For unless a truce were arranged soon, the militants stood an excellent chance of gaining control of Parliament. And if this should occur then the war would be carried on interminably, resulting in the shattering of the whole fabric of English government and society. Because of this very real threat, which increased as the war continued, Charles must agree to any terms offered at this time. Once peace was achieved, both Holles and Whitelock felt confident that men of good will in Parliament would see to it that the king's sovereignty was largely restored. The two men also argued that if Charles accepted the proposals and returned to London, he would be certain to win back the sympathy of the English populace.[13]

Holles and Whitelock also advised the king to be more cordial to the Scottish commissioners, who, they claimed, were favorable disposed to the idea of retaining a strong English monarch. The Scots, Charles was informed, actually gave signs of moderating their religious demands; in fact, they might even consent to a church government not strictly *jure divino.* Why Charles should have been impressed by this announcement of Scottish generosity remains a bit of a mystery. The point Whitelock and Holles seem to have been making here was simply that the king had more sympathizers in the Parliamentary ranks than he realized. As soon as he should demonstrate his moderation, support would come in from various quarters. Thus the one message they reiterated throughout their private meeting with him was that he should accept the present treaty and return to London.[14]

There can be no question that Charles benefited from the advice given him by Holles and Whitelock. Evidently he took it into serious consideration, and one might even see ways in which it influenced his policy. Hence, instead of rejecting Parliament's offer outright, as some of his advisers suggested, Charles decided to demonstrate a willingness to negotiate. He sent off two Royalists, the Duke of Richmond and the Earl of Southampton, to London for the purpose of arranging a formal series of talks on the basis of Parliament's proposals,[15] which represented a sizable concession on his part. In effect, therefore, the initiative for the later negotiations at Uxbridge came from Charles.

While the king demonstrated an interest in certain ideas put forward by the peace party, he most definitely did not accept their gloomy prognostication for the future. If anything, recent events enabled him to be more optimistic about his own state of affairs. On November 9, just a fortnight before the Parliamentary Commissioners arrived in Oxford, the Royalists succeeded in relieving Donnington Castle, while it was being besieged by a combined Roundhead force. More important than the actual victory was the fact that their failure had a disuniting effect on the leadership of Parliament's armies. For in his wake at Donnington Castle, the king left behind a dispirited group of squabbling and disgruntled generals.

In repose after the successful engagement, Charles examined his position vis-à-vis Parliament's, and concluded that his cause had been greatly revived. In a letter written in December to his queen, Charles observed:

> I am put in very good hope (some hold it a certainty) that if I could come to a fair treaty, the ring leading rebels could not hinder me from a good peace; first, because their own party are most weary of the war, and likewise for the great distractions which at this time most assuredly are amongst themselves, as Presbyterians against Independents in religion, and general against general in point of command: upon these grounds a treaty being most desirable (not without hope of good success).[16]

The king had in fact put his finger on Parliament's main problem. The divisions opened up within their ranks after the poor showing at Donnington Castle, and also at Newbury, appeared to be very sharp indeed. If this disunity continued, Parliament could hardly plan on having an effective army in the field by the next spring's campaign. As the Venetian ambassador perceived, "the army, amid its hardships, without pay and without leaders, is going to ruin." [17] Aggravating the present quandary was the long-standing, smoldering controversy between Cromwell and the Earl of Manchester, which had never been fully resolved.

When Manchester took his leave of London in September, he promised that he would press on with the war. "You need not fear any disagreement on my part in point of command," he wrote the Committee of Both

Kingdoms on the 22nd. But within a week the committee had to prod him to hasten his march westward.[18] By October 2 the directives from Derby House became even more insistent: Manchester should move forward "with all expedition, that we shall not need to reiterate them again to your Lordship." [19] A week later Whitacre reported that

> twelve or fourteen letters were shown to the House from the Committee of Both Kingdoms, which they had sent to the Earl of Manchester to go on with his force westward to join with Sir William Waller, and the House seemed to marvel much at his advancing no further.[20]

On October 19 the Earl of Manchester at long last joined forces with Sir William Waller. Eight days later the combined armies engaged the Royalists at the second battle of Newbury. The outcome of this encounter proved indecisive, mainly because at a key moment during the engagement Manchester hesitated to give the command to attack.[21] After the battle itself, a second lapse by Manchester enabled the king to recover vital arms and artillery which could easily have been captured. When the news of these events reached London, the Committee of Both Kingdoms proclaimed them a serious setback, even a dishonor, for Parliament's army. Moreover, with their troops much reduced in number, exhausted by the unusually bad weather, and inadequately supplied, it was no wonder that the commanders felt completely demoralized.[22]

Previously when Cromwell challenged Manchester's leadership, he directed his venom against advisers like Major General Crawford. In September, at the time of the first rift, Cromwell chose not to divide the Eastern Association's army in view of the fact that two or three more months of the campaign still remained. By the end of November he saw no further reason to act with circumspection. Parliament's entire force was in a state of collapse, and the situation could hardly have been more critical. If he wanted a major source of Parliament's difficulties to be uncovered and removed, Cromwell knew that he must now take on the man whom he held responsible. Accordingly, when he received a request from the Commons to give an account of "the particular proceeding of the armies since their conjunction," he was provided with a platform ideally suited for condemnation of his superior officer.[23]

On the 25th of November Cromwell delivered a blistering speech to the Commons, putting forward his case against the Earl of Manchester, whom he held accountable for every mishap that had befallen their army since the taking of York. The substance of his argument rested on the charge that the earl no longer wished to defeat the king.

> And because I had a great deal of reason to think that his Lordship's miscarriage in these particulars was neither through accidents (which could not be helped), nor through his improvidence only, but through his backwardness; was not (merely) from dullness or indisposedness to engagement, but (withal) for some principle of unwillingness in his Lordship to have this war prosecuted into a full victory, and a design or desire to have it ended by accommodation, (and that) on such terms to which it might be disadvantageous to bring the King too low.[24]

Cromwell's narrative of the recent campaign created a sensation, the reverberations of which lasted for months afterward. In addition to being a devastating assault on the general of the Eastern Association's army, the address contained a warning for the future. For Cromwell's speech cannot be fully appreciated if it is viewed only as a personal attack on Manchester; it must also be seen as a complaint against all other Parliamentary generals of a moderate stamp, who, like Manchester, advocated a negotiated peace. Parliament, Cromwell argued by implication, could no longer afford to place its troops under the command of officers who were not committed to victory. If Parliament wished to continue the struggle against the prelates and Papists, changes must be made in the leadership of their army. Thus, while his name was not mentioned, the Earl of Essex had to be considered by innuendo a Manchester writ large.[25]

This speech reveals also how political orientations in Parliament had grown more radical over the past several months. In holding Manchester's opposition to total victory up for derision, Cromwell must have expected a large segment of the Commons to join him in condemning the earl. Yet surely Manchester's views on a negotiated peace had once been widely advocated. In fact, they had been perfectly orthodox middle-group policy during the previous year, while Pym lived. Cromwell's attack on peace by accommodation in November 1644 thus provides us with further evidence of how the middle group had declined in importance over the past year.

The Earl of Manchester asked permission of the House of Lords to reply to Cromwell, and on the 28th he delivered his own narration of events.[26] A large portion of the earl's speech provided the peers with some shocking instances of his lieutenant's irreverence. According to Manchester, Cromwell hated the nobility, had contempt for the Assembly of Divines, and at all costs opposed peace. Moreover, Cromwell frequently expressed his complete and utter disdain for the Scots and their Presbyterian church.

> His animosity was such as he told me that in the way they now carried themselves, pressing for their discipline, he could as soon draw his sword against them as against any in the King's army.[27]

The Lords requested Manchester to put his charges against Cromwell into writing, and when he completed this task they appointed a committee of Lords to join with the Commons for the purpose of investigating *his* charges—not Cromwell's. But three days earlier the Commons had stolen the Lords' thunder by referring the question of Cromwell's accusations "to the examination of the committee formerly appointed for my Lord General's army where Mr. Tate has the chair."[28] And from November 25 until January 6 this committee heard testimony from practically every ranking officer, including Waller, Haselrig, Ireton, Lilburne, and many others.[29] The conflicting approaches taken by the two houses set off an additional controversy. Each house took the side of its own member in the dispute, but the Commons went a step further. They conceived "the privilege of the house to be broken by the Lords in going about to make a charge against a Member of our house," as Whitacre explained it.[30]

If the newsbooks of the time accurately reflect attitudes in Parliament, then the disclosures by both Cromwell and Manchester must have been greatly distressing. As we have frequently noted, a large number of members of Parliament always sought to avoid controversies that created disunity. They believed that quarrels that served to weaken the cause must be dropped at all costs. Until this juncture in the war, the leaders of Parliament had managed to reconcile differences, no matter how sharp; but this particular trouble appeared to be getting out of control. Consequently, we find the *Parliamentary Scout* commenting on the controversy as follows:

> We pray it may be all buried in the grave of oblivion, and though there be many reasons for that prayer, yet there is enough, the Royal party are so much joy'd in our division, and make themselves confident that that will bring about a peace to their mind.[31]

And *Mercurius Britanicus* must have summed up the sentiments of many when it warned: "A plot from Oxford could have done no more, than work a distance between our best resolved spirits." [32]

While responsible members of Parliament became deeply concerned about the divisions caused by the growing animosities, and sought to reduce tensions, the Scots reacted in the opposite manner. This is a curious development, for the Covenanters had always been advocates of Parliamentary unity and had preached conciliation even more emphatically since September. But they drew the line when the object of the dispute was their *bête noire,* Oliver Cromwell. Very understandably, they were deeply offended by accounts of his alleged remarks concerning Scotland. They began to interpret the struggle as essentially a religious one between the Independents led by Cromwell, and the Presbyterians represented by those opposing him. Their sympathies lay with Manchester, whom they conceived to be fighting Independency. Baillie's violent reaction to recent events reflected Scottish opinion. "The matter of Cromwell," he wrote,

> has been a high and mighty plot of the Independent party to have gotten an army for themselves under Cromwell, with the ruin and shamefully unjust crushing of Manchester's person, of dissolving the

> union of the nations, of abolishing the House of Lords, of dividing the House of Commons, of felling this city, and most of the Commons, with intestine wars, of setting up themselves on the ruins of all.[33]

A prime object of Scottish policy would henceforth be the removal of Oliver Cromwell from a position where he might do them harm.

The desire of the Scots to rid themselves of "that darling of the sectaries" was shared by his enemies in Parliament, mainly peace-party men. The Marquis of Sabran had long been anxious to arrange an alliance between the pacific members and the Scots, but without any success to date. He now saw his opportunity, for both parties regarded Cromwell as a menace, and might be willing to combine forces against him. It was still too early for a formal alliance, as differences over ultimate goals remained sharp. Yet on this occasion the interests of the two groups coincided so powerfully that it seemed especially desirable for them to work together. The Scots took the initiative and called for a meeting so that a plan of action could be drawn up. Among the Scots, the Earl of Loudoun played a leading role; while the Earl of Essex, Sir Philip Stapleton, and Denzil Holles represented the peace party.[34]

Meeting together, the two parties decided that the best approach was to have Cromwell tried as an incendiary, as defined by the terms of the Solemn League and Covenant. The fact that he slandered the Scots, thereby helping to damage the Anglo-Scottish alliance, would be the grounds on which they hoped to base a conviction. Before proceeding, however, prudence dictated that they should receive expert legal advice. Late one evening, during the first days of December 1644, John Maynard and Bulstrode Whitelock received a summons to come to the residence of the Earl of Essex.[35] Here they found a house crowded with Scottish commissioners and peace-group men. Without much of an introduction the Earl of Loudoun asked the two lawyers whether, according to English practice, there existed sufficient grounds to act against Cromwell. The cautious Whitelock answered first with great circumspection.

Called in to give his opinion upon a question of law, Whitelock concentrated his attention upon practical realities rather than on the legal complexities of the case. He told the Scots and the Lord General that they, as "persons of so great honor and authority," should be hesitant against bringing action unless they could be absolutely certain of the outcome. To risk a confrontation with Cromwell, while possessing only inconclusive evidence to back up their charge, might result in a political setback for the peace party and a great victory for their opponents. In clear and straightforward language, Whitelock enumerated those present political facts which tended to work against the anti-Cromwell forces.

> I take Lt. General Cromwell to be a gentleman of quick and subtle parts, and one who hath (especially of late) gained no small interest in the House of Commons, nor is he wanting of friends in the House of Lords, nor of abilities in himself to manage his own part or defense to the best advantage.

When his turn came, John Maynard agreed fully with Whitelock, only adding more emphasis to his colleague's argument. Apparently their joint presentation made an impression upon the Scots, who concluded that the two men had analyzed the situation correctly. Although Holles and Stapleton would have preferred to press on against Cromwell, the Scots began to withdraw their support for the scheme.[36] They still wished to see Cromwell removed from the army, but were unwilling to risk the eventuality of a calamitous humiliation which might do irreparable damage to their cause.

While the Scots and the peace group searched for a means to blunt the threat posed by Cromwell, and while the neutral members of Parliament sought to end the great disunity that had befallen the army, the war party was at work devising a measure to satisfy all factions. Throughout the Civil War, as we have often observed, a prime goal of the militants had been to put together any army that could bring victory. In the past they had suffered disillusionment with several champions, including Sir William Waller, the Earl of Manchester, and finally the entire Scottish army. Now, in December 1644, to rid Parliament of those ineffectual and politically undesirable officers who did not really seek a military solution to the war became their immediate goal. To remove a general from a position of command was no easy task, as they already knew. But while they racked their brains for a way to revive the army, one of the militants (whether Vane, St. John, Cromwell, or another is impossible to say) concocted a most original design—one that would assure the war party's aim of eliminating the moderate military leaders. The price to be paid for such a triumph was that Cromwell himself would have to sacrifice his command, along with the other generals.[37] This was the dramatic piece of legislation later known as the "Self-Denying Ordinance," which retired all members of Parliament, Lords and Commons alike, from positions of command or profit.

The ingenuity of the war party's plan must be seen in historical context to be truly appreciated. Despite its seemingly spontaneous character, the idea for a Self-Denying Ordinance did not suddenly spring full blown from the brow of Zouch Tate on December 9. Just a year previously, on December 12, 1643, the House of Lords had moved "that this house would declare it as the opinion of this house, that no Members of either house of Parliament might be admitted or execute any places of profit." [38] Nothing more had been heard of this motion until October 1644, when the Commons requested the Committee of Privileges "to consider what Members of this house are in public service, or otherwise, and to bring in a list of them, and of what nature their employments are." [39] Fifteen days later a committee consisting largely of peace-party men like Holles, Stapleton, Clotworthy, Reynolds, Whitelock, and others, was called upon

> to inquire into the value and nature of all the offices and places, and other advantages that have been bestowed by the Parliament, or by virtue or color of any authority of Parliament; what is received by the persons on whom such offices, places or other advantages are bestowed . . . and are to begin first with the offices, places or other advantages bestowed upon members of either house.

The order named Robert Reynolds "especially to take care of this business." [40]

The singling out of Reynolds for the chairmanship of the committee seems to indicate that he himself sponsored the order. One might even suggest that the concept of a "self-denying" ordinance had been created by the peace group to embarrass the war party. For by claiming that members of Parliament made profit out of the war, Reynolds cast serious doubts on the motives of those who called for greater militancy against Charles. Such a charge was a stick with which the peace party might beat their rivals. Nor did these accusations fade away to be forgotten; they were to be revived again and again throughout the war. Thus when Tate, Cromwell, and Vane came to speak about the greed among "certain" M.P.s, they would be repeating charges long familiar to their listeners.[41]

The 9th of December had been selected as the day for presenting the report by the committee dealing with the Cromwell-Manchester dispute. Zouch Tate, the chairman of this committee and a Presbyterian member of the war party, began the debate. The lower house was filled and an air of expectancy hovered over the assemblage, for the day's proceedings might very well determine Parliament's future conduct of the Civil War. Tate, conscious of the seriousness of the occasion, chose to appeal to emotions instead of dealing with the specifics of Cromwell's charges. He would not dwell on the errors of a few men, but upon the common sins of all. "The chief causes of our division," confessed the pious Tate, "are pride and covetousness."[42] He was quickly followed by the equally contrite Cromwell, who agreed with the previous speaker and carried the same argument one step further. "I hope," he proclaimed,

> we have such true English hearts and zealous affections towards the general weal of our mother country, as no Members of either house will scruple to deny themselves and their own private interests for the public good.[43]

A lengthy debate ensued on the theme struck by Tate and Cromwell, i.e., "touching the Members of the house that had any offices of command in any of the army, or any office in civil affairs either judicial or ministerial."[44] Later in the discussion Zouch Tate again took the floor to propose the famous motion:

> that during the time of this war no Member of either house shall have or execute any office or command, military or civil, granted or conferred by both or either of the houses of Parliament.

The motion was immediately seconded by Sir Henry Vane, Jr., who, with a dramatic gesture, offered to surrender his position as co-treasurer of the navy.[45] The excitement generated by this revolutionary proposal must have been enormous, for it appeared that Parliament now possessed the magic formula by which all its troubles could be made to disappear. Furthermore, those members who feared either a victorious army with Cromwell at the helm or a dispirited force under Essex, saw their remedy right at hand. With one swift blow all the squabbling officers, Essex and Waller, Cromwell and Manchester, would be quickly removed. The motion introduced by Tate received an enthusiastic approbation, and with this momentum behind it, the measure was sent off to committee.[46]

The perfect solution provided by the Self-Denying Ordinance met with almost universal public endorsement. All the London newsbooks added their approving voices to the growing chorus of acclaim. The *Scottish Dove,* the paper which most nearly reflected the official Scottish position, was as warm to the measure as any of the London weeklies. The *Dove* wrote editorially: "In this vote, more differences are reconciled at once than a whole year could have ended." [47] And if Baillie is once again taken as representing the opinion of the Scottish commissioners, then they too responded favorably to an ordinance that promised to remove the chief threat to their policies. After discussing the merits of the measure Baillie concluded, "We pray God it may have a good success." [48]

Not all Parliamentarians viewed the Self-Denying Ordinance with such esteem. From the start the peace group regarded the measure as just one more episode in the year-long campaign to remove the Earl of Essex from a position of command. Whitelock, for instance, saw the whole affair as a plot contrived by the "violent spirits" for the purpose of "ousting of the Lord General, and to bring on their own designs." He claimed that members of the war party had confessed their scheme to him:

> and it was apparent in itself, the reason of their doing this was to make way for others, and because they were jealous that the Lord General was too much a favorer of peace.[49]

The leaders of the peace group countered the altruistic protestations of

Cromwell and Vane with charges of hypocrisy. Though some nonaligned members considered the exchange of Essex's resignation for Cromwell's to be an equitable quid pro quo, the peace party certainly did not. Cromwell was merely a lieutenant general in the army of the Eastern Association, while the Earl of Essex still held his post as Lord General of the entire army.

On the 17th of December the peace party made a last-ditch attempt within the Commons to save Essex from his appointed fate. Robert Reynolds proposed an amendment excluding Essex from the terms of the Self-Denying Ordinance. Following a debate, which we are told lasted the whole day, Reynolds's motion was rejected by only seven votes out of 193 cast.[50] Thus, after a year and one-half, the war party finally succeeded in convincing the Commons to retire the Lord General. Nevertheless, the sizable vote in his favor demonstrated what strong loyalty he still commanded, especially among some of the noncommitted members.[51] No doubt the state of Parliament's military forces and the disunity among the generals contributed to Essex's defeat. The majority who carried against the earl represented not only those in the war party who distrusted him, but also a large body of neutrals. Men like John Crew and William Pierrepoint supported the measure because they saw its passage as the only means of escaping the present impasse.[52]

Naturally enough, the House of Lords refused to swallow the Self-Denying Ordinance whole. If passed, the measure would not only automatically reduce the importance of the Lords by eliminating them from key posts, it would also serve to abolish the ancient right of the peers to these high offices of state. When the ordinance was first sent up to them on December 19, the upper house chose to ignore it completely. But after twenty-five days of procrastination, they finally rejected it outright.[53]

On the surface this negative reaction would appear to have represented a serious setback for the House of Commons, and especially for the war party. But oddly enough, the Lords' vote did not have any appreciable effect on future events. As far as the Commons were concerned, the passage of the ordinance by their House was all that mattered; they regarded the Lords' ratification as a formality which might be dispensed with. True, they badgered the Lords on several occasions, even threatening to revive charges against Manchester if the upper house failed to comply (a threat never carried out). But for all practical purposes the Commons chose to forget that the Lords played any role in legislation, and proceeded as if the proposed Self-Denying Ordinance had in fact become law.[54] A precedent for circumventing the House of Lords had been set the previous May when the Committee of Both Kingdoms was renewed essentially without the Lords' approval.[55]

At the very time that the Lords pondered the dangerous precedent inherent in barring peers from office, the Commons set out to reorganize the army. Anyone concerned with the breakdown in the military structure recognized that a drastic overhauling of the entire establishment was required if Parliament hoped to field an effective fighting force by the spring. The present army had all but disintegrated. The troops were terribly demoralized, large numbers of soldiers deserted their units, and those who remained suffered extreme hardships. Much of the trouble stemmed from the inadequate arrangements for pay and supplies, a lacuna in Parliament's armor which had been only too apparent during the ill-fated Newbury campaign, when unpaid militia men fled their ranks en masse. On November 23 the House of Commons acknowledged the necessity for a drastic reorganization by requesting the Committee of Both Kingdoms "to consider of a frame or model of the whole militia." [56]

The matter of remodeling Parliament's armies required a month's consideration before the committee completed its labors, and sent off to the Commons the draft of an ordinance. In spite of its revolutionary character the measure met with instant approval. Nor did the fact that the "violent spirits," especially Vane and Cromwell, had played a leading part in framing the ordinance interfere with its acclaim.[57]

In brief, the New Model devised by the Committee of Both Kingdoms provided for a national army under direct Parliamentary supervision, rather than a series of local ones subject to the whims of various county associations. Designed to consist of 21,000 men, the army would be paid from monthly assessments levied on individual counties. They would be imposed on a regular basis by authority of Parliament. The outstanding feature of the ordinance was that it centralized Parliament's entire military organization, an absolute necessity in order to eliminate the handicaps that had hamstrung the army in the past. If the new units could take shape within a few months, then Parliament might very well have created the force that would bring final victory.[58]

Since the proposal for a New Model Army represented the only available path out of the present morass, a majority in the Commons, including many neutrals, came out overwhelmingly in its favor; and the legislation passed the lower house on January 11 without a division. The favorable reaction accorded the New Model was again demonstrated ten days later, when the Committee of Both Kingdoms recommended the appointment of Sir Thomas Fairfax as its Lord General. This matter was a crucial one indeed; for if Sir Thomas were appointed, the Earl of Essex would no longer hold any position in the army. The ordinance did not specifically deny Essex his command, it ignored his existence, which amounted to the same thing. Determining Essex's future proved controversial enough to force a division on Fairfax's appointment, but out of 170 votes cast, 101 supported Fairfax, giving him a safe margin of thirty-two.[59] The Commons then proceeded to appoint Philip Skippon as major general of the foot, while the name of the lieutenant general of the horse was mysteriously left blank.[60]

Sir Thomas Fairfax, Parliament's choice as commander in chief of the army, was a man whose views on politics and religion were as great an enigma to contemporaries as they are to us today. His failure to commit himself on the issues of the day (apart from his general support of Parliament) undoubtedly helped his career. Certainly the fact that he never became embroiled in the controversies, which few generals avoided, allowed him to come forth as the one man who stood unmarred by criticisms and jealousies. He excelled as a leader of men more by his example of bravery (his recent arm wound testified to this) than by any outstanding command of military strategy. Undoubtedly the strongest point in Sir Thomas's favor in January 1645 was that he did not sit in Parliament.[61]

The Lords opposed the Self-Denying Ordinance because they did not want Essex or other nobles removed from their positions. But the New Model Ordinance presented them with a serious dilemma. They could not reject it without jeopardizing Parliament's military standing irreparably. Yet if they assented to the New Model Army with Fairfax at its head, they would by implication admit the necessity for the Self-Denying Ordinance as well. In the atmosphere of desperation prevalent in the winter of 1644-1645, the Lords had no choice. They knew that a categorical rejection of the new army would heap such opprobrium upon them that their very existence might be threatened. Consequently, they were forced to ratify the legislation for the remodeling of Parliament's military force. By so doing, however, the Lords accepted the principle of their own exclusion from office.

Once the upper house began to show some willingness to adopt the New Model Ordinance, the Commons allowed them the luxury of a few isolated modifications. The Lords did actually hit on one point which proved a sore one for the Commons; they wanted to prevent members of religious sects who had been with Cromwell in the Eastern Association army from obtaining high ranks in the New Model. In their endeavor to reduce the number of Cromwell's allies in the army, the Lords achieved a measure of success. Here they had the support of those neutrals in the lower house who did not wish to see the religious Independents and other sectarians gain military control. Thus, a qualification added to the original draft specifically stated that all commanders and officers "shall take the National League and Covenant of both Kingdoms, within 20 days." If anyone refused, he "shall not be admitted to any office or command." A second qualification appended by the Lords provided that all officers above the rank of sergeant major, nominated by the commander in chief, must be approved by both houses of Parliament. These two stipulations were allowed to stand in the final version of the ordinance for a New Model Army, which became law on February 17.[62]

Despite the minor annoyance of having to grant a few concessions to the Lords, the passage of the ordinance for the army must be regarded as a smashing victory for the war party and a significant setback for the peace group. And one of the reasons that the war party had such an easy time achieving their aims was that they encountered no opposition from the Scottish commissioners.

NOTES

1. Clarendon, III, p. 453.
2. Meikle, pp. 38-39.
3. C.J., III, p. 659. This indicated that the godly party was still intact.
4. *Instructions,* June 28, 1644.
5. Meikle, p. 45.
6. Denzil Holles wrote in his *Memoirs:* "By little and little the Scots and these [the peace party] came to a better understanding" (p. 21).
7. D.A. Digby, "The Relations between England and France during the Great Rebellion," unpublished M.A. thesis, London University, 1912, *passim.*
8. Sabran, 5460, fols. 215v-216.
9. Ibid., fol. 283v.
10. Whitelock, *Memorials,* II, pp. 334-336.
11. Sabran, 5460, fols. 215v-216.
12. L.J., VII, pp. 82-83; Whitelock, II, p. 333.
13. The details of this secret meeting are given in Whitelock, *Memorials,* II, pp. 334-336, 462-464; and in the MSS of his *Annals,* Add. MSS, 37,343, fol. 340. See also Burnet, *History of His Own Time,* I, pp. 38-39, where Burnet reported a conversation with Holles. In his *Annals* Whitelock delivered to his children an account of the secret meeting, and then went on to say: "And here I have discoursed to you these secret and private passages which we do not impart to our fellow Commissioners, and which all the examinations at committee in the House of Commons could not get out of us" (fol. 340).
14. Whitelock, II, pp. 334-336.
15. C.J., III, p. 710.
16. The King's Cabinet, T.T., E. 292 (27).
17. C.S.P. Ven., p. 159.

18. C.S.P.D., 1644, pp. 526, 541.
19. Ibid., 1644-45, pp. 4-5.
20. Whitacre, fol. 330.
21. Austin Woolrych, *Battles of the English Civil War* (London, 1961), p. 85.
22. C.S.P.D., 1644-45, pp. 118, 125. For a recent account of this campaign, as well as a full discussion of the background, see Clive Holmes, *The Eastern Association in the Civil War* (Cambridge, England, 1974).
23. C.J., III, p. 703.
24. Abbott, I, p. 302.
25. Professor Holmes makes an interesting case for the proposition that after Newbury the Earl of Essex tried to denigrate all the other Parliamentary generals so that he might reassert his former supremacy in the army (op. cit., p. 208). But this hypothesis minimizes Cromwell's attack on all peace-oriented generals (now including Manchester). Nor does it explain why, shortly after his November 25 speech, Essex sought ways to remove only Cromwell. Thus Whitelock wrote at this time "that the Lord General now began to have some jealousies" of Cromwell (II, p. 343).
26. L.J., VIII, p. 76.
27. *Camden Miscellany,* vol. VIII (London, 1883), p. 2.
28. L.J., VIII, p. 79; C.J., III, p. 704.
29. C.S.P.D., 1644-45, pp. 146-147.
30. Whitacre, fol. 355.
31. *Parliamentary Scout,* November 25, 1644.
32. *Mercurius Britanicus,* December 9, 1644.
33. Baillie, II, p. 246.
34. Whitelock, II, pp. 343-344.
35. Ibid., pp. 344-347; for all that follows regarding the meeting.
36. Ibid., pp. 346-347.
37. The historian S. R. Gardiner cannot bring himself to believe that his hero, Oliver Cromwell, could have been involved in such devious machinations. See *Civil War,* II, pp. 90-92. Gardiner feels that there was no collusion between Tate, a Presbyterian, and Cromwell, an Independent. But in reality these members of the war party had a

common interest in victory over the king, and both favored a reformation of the army.

38. L.J., VI, p. 338. G. E. Aylmer in his article, "Place Bills and the Separation of Powers," *Transactions of the Royal Historical Society,* fifth series, vol. XV (1965), pp. 45-69, discusses some of the forerunners of the Self-Denying Ordinance.
39. C.J., III, p. 683.
40. Ibid., p. 695.
41. Cromwell directed himself to these charges in one of his speeches on December 9 (Rushworth, VI, p. 4).
42. Whitacre, fol. 356. The fact that Tate chose to give this type of speech rather than one that dealt with Cromwell's specific points raises the question of his collusion with the war party. Undoubtedly his speech created a mood that Vane and Cromwell could exploit.
43. Rushworth, VI, p. 4.
44. Whitacre, fol. 356.
45. C.J., III, p. 718; Abbott, I, p. 315. The speed with which Vane jumped on the bandwagon also casts doubt upon the spontaneous nature of the Self-Denying Ordinance. It is stretching credibility to suggest that a man of Vane's experience would second such a sweeping motion on the spur of the moment, without any forethought.
46. C.J., III, p. 718.
47. *Scottish Dove,* December 13, 1644; *Mercurius Britanicus,* December 9, 1644.
48. Baillie, II, p. 247.
49. Whitelock, II, p. 349.
50. C.J. III, p. 726; Whitacre, fol. 359.
51. Clarendon tells us that Sir William Waller, Walter Long, and John Glyn voted for Essex (Clarendon, III, p. 507).
52. *Vindiciae Veritatis,* 1654, T.T., E., 811 (2), part I, p. 52. *Mercurius Britanicus* in an "editorial" on December 30, 1644 presented the view of these neutrals: "Doubt–What may be a main hindrance to the proceeding of our army? Satisfaction–Delay in despatch of the grand ordinance for exempting the Members of both Houses from their

offices, military or civil." Clarendon, III, p. 508, lists the names of supporters of the Self-Denying Ordinance, but he must be read with care. For example, he cites Whitelock as a supporter, although we know that the latter opposed the measure. See Whitelock, II, pp. 352-355. Also, Clarendon speaks of St. John as a member of the Earl of Essex's party, whereas he had opposed Essex for at least a year. See Dewes, 165, fols. 266-266v.

53. L.J., VIII, pp. 135-136.
54. *Weekly Account,* January 21, 1645, makes a similar point.
55. See above, chap. II.
56. C.J., III, p. 703.
57. *Mercurius Aulicus,* January 12, 1645.
58. *Acts and Ordinances,* I, pp. 614-626.
59. C.J., IV, p. 26.
60. Whether this failure to name a general of the horse was an oversight, or intentionally done, is a subject of controversy among historians. Interpretations depend largely on one's analysis of Cromwell. My own guess is that the place was left open as a threat to the Lords. If they did not accept the Self-Denying Ordinance, Cromwell could always be chosen for the spot.
61. D.N.B.
62. *Acts and Ordinances,* I, pp. 614-626. John Lilburne, among others, surrendered his commission because of the required oath.

IV

The Uxbridge Treaty and Its Consequences

From the time they dropped their anti-Cromwell scheme, the Covenanters had stayed out of internal political conflicts, continuing to pursue their middle-party line; "that either by treaty or by a powerful war, we shall have such a safe and honorable peace," as the commissioners described it.[1] When this passage was written on December 23, 1944, the Scots had placed all their hopes on a successful treaty with the king. Consequently, they observed the struggle over the New Model Ordinance from a distance, and did not commit themselves.[2] Perhaps if they had joined forces with the peace group, the outcome would have been more favorable for the moderates. But the Covenanters chose not to do anything to oppose the creation of the New Model Army, nor did they lift a finger to save Essex.

The chief concern of the Scots at this moment was the approaching negotiations with the king, and they gave their full attention to this project. The Venetian ambassador described in several of his letters, written in January, how they worked constantly in preparation for the treaty. On the 20th Agostini wrote, "The efforts of the Scottish Commissioners for peace [are] backed by the Lords, who seek this way to avoid the ruin with which they are threatened." [3] The Covenanters now regarded peace as the panacea for all their problems; yet ironically, they themselves contributed more to the collapse of the treaty than any other party.

The paradoxical role played by the Scots remains one of the strangest aspects of the whole Civil War. Most of the difficulty experienced by them during their involvement in the war stemmed from the illusions they continued to hold regarding an English religious settlement. Despite all evidence to the contrary, the Covenanters persisted in their belief that they could pressure the English into establishing a church similar in form and spirit to their own. They also conceived that, given the chance, Charles might be convinced to renounce episcopacy and accept Presbyterianism in its stead.

Already in the autumn of 1644 the Scots had stepped up their campaign to hasten the Westminster Assembly and Parliament along the road to a Presbyterian church. The Scottish divines in London continued to pray for a military success which would strengthen their bargaining position. Disappointed by what they regarded as Cromwell's usurpation of the honors after Marston Moor, they were forced to wait patiently for a purely Scottish victory. Finally, after what seemed an excessive delay, the Scottish army on October 19, 1644 took the city of Newcastle. Full of self-congratulations, the Scottish generals sent off a letter to London, "pressing the expediting the settling of the affairs of the church for preventing the growth of sectaries and schismatics." [4]

A week after Newcastle fell to the Covenanters, the Assembly of Divines presented Parliament with "their humble advice" concerning the future church government. A few of the Scottish divines accompanied the group, which consisted largely of English Presbyterians. The ministers attempted to use the momentum of the recent victory to establish definitively that Presbyterianism was *jure divino.* Knowing full well that a majority in Parliament rejected this concept, these shrewd clerics brought their advice to the Commons early in the morning, before all the members had arrived. Fortunately for the non-Presbyterians, John Glyn and Bulstrode Whitelock were themselves early risers, and proceeded to wax eloquent on sundry matters long enough for the house to fill. When they finally relinquished the floor, there were sufficient members present to put aside the question of *jure divino* for an indefinite period.[5]

Although the Scottish clergymen did not succeed in having all the ingredients of a Presbyterian church accepted by Parliament, they did receive the satisfaction of seeing a completion favorable to themselves. On January 4, 1645 an ordinance passed both houses abolishing the Book of Common Prayer and establishing a Directory of Public Worship in its place.[6] At the same time their opponents, the dissenting brethren, began to find the House of Commons less responsive to their needs. When the Independents, on December 23, presented elaborate arguments against presbyterial government, the lower house specified that only 300 copies of the Independent statement should be printed, and once this was done, Parliament proceeded to ignore the whole question of dissenting religious views.[7]

Another hopeful sign for the Scots occurred in January when Parliament decided to hasten the settlement of the church along Presbyterian lines. On the 14th of the month the Commons resolved that "many particular congregations may be under one Presbyterial government." A week later they put on record that the future church would be

> governed by congregational, classical and synodical assemblies, in such manner as shall be established by Parliament;

and also

> that synodical assemblies shall consist of both provincial and national assemblies.[8]

While the foregoing provisions by no means acknowledged Presbyterianism as *jure divino,* they did go a considerable way toward creating a Presbyterian church of sorts in England. As a result, the Scots began to feel more optimistic, and with good cause; these resolutions would soon be presented to the king at Uxbridge as part of Parliament's proposed treaty.[9]

The question to which we must now address ourselves is: Why did Parliament begin to favor a Presbyterian settlement? Those historians who believe that the Independents dominated Parliament at this time are hard put to explain the acceptance of the Presbyterian tenets quoted above.[10] The fact of the matter is that only a handful of men in the Commons during the winter of 1644-1645 can accurately be classified as religious Independents. Baillie himself realized this fact: "Of those who joined with the Parliament, the greatest and most countenanced part were much Episcopal." [11]

While definitely an exaggeration, Baillie's observation possessed a certain validity. He was correct in assuming that neither the Independents nor the Presbyterians had a large body of adherents in the Long Parliament. But there could also be no doubt that a vast majority rejected Laudian episcopacy, which conjured up recollections of "eleven years of tyranny." What Parliament sought, at this time, was a church settlement which would place ultimate control in its hands, rather than with the king; and this would require the kind of centralized organization provided by a modified Presbyterianism. Two important features would characterize English Presbyterianism. The placing of Parliament at the apogee of the ecclesiastical structure would be the first, while a second was its flexible and fluid character, which made it subject to change whenever Parliament should desire.

For the Scots, the act symbolizing the abolition of episcopacy was the execution of Archbishop Laud. The archbishop had been in the Tower since March 1, 1641, but his trial did not really begin until three years later.[12] At a certain point his prosecutors realized that he would most certainly be acquitted on a treason charge. They then began thinking in terms of an ordinance of attainder. That the House of Commons would proceed in this fashion became clear in the early part of November 1644, when Laud was asked to appear before them. Behind the Commons, pressing for Laud's execution at every opportunity, stood the Scots. When the lower house finally drew up the attainder ordinance, Sabran recognized that "Laud was condemned to death for the Scots' benefit." [13]

From the middle of November until early January the Commons, led by Oliver St. John and William Strode, bombarded the Lords with the demand that the upper house accept the attainder measure. On January 4 their badgering accomplished the desired effect: a reduced House of Lords reluctantly agreed to ratify the ordinance,[14] and six days later Laud was beheaded.

The Scots had wished to rid themselves of the archbishop before the sessions at Uxbridge began in earnest. They had called for his death, as *Mercurius Aulicus* understood, on the grounds that "things in Scotland could never remain secure if Canterbury were left alive." [15] But the Scots could hardly have chosen a less opportune time for the deed. The execution of his former adviser and head of his church could only serve to harden Charles against an accommodation. Peter Heylyn, the Anglican minister, commenting on the timing of Laud's death, wrote: "This could presage no good success to the following treaty. For though covenants sometimes may be writ in blood, yet I find no such way for commencing treaties." [16] And from Clarendon: "It was, as is said before, a very sad omen to the treaty." [17]

A worse omen for the treaty was, of course, its terms, which the Scots, encouraged by the war party, had helped to devise.[18] As Charles recognized, Parliament's proposals in effect required the king to surrender his religion, almost all of his sovereignty, and many of his closest friends and advisers. He would be asked to void the cessation in Ireland, a demand which carried the implication that he had not possessed the authority, moral or legal, to grant it in the first place. Furthermore, the treaty carried provision for the creation of a joint commission, composed of Scots and English, to meet at regular intervals for the purpose of directing the military affairs of both kingdoms and preventing "the violation of the articles of peace." Included in these articles was the stipulation that the Scots would continue to direct the war in Ireland.[19] During the negotiations at Uxbridge, Parliament further clarified its position concerning the settling of the militia. On February 21 the two houses ordered that the militia would continue under their direction for three years after the peace, "or for seven years at least from the time of the passing of the act for the militia." [20]

Without doubt, the treaty offered by Parliament and their Scottish allies had almost no chance of gaining the king's acceptance. The utter futility of the Uxbridge negotiations became apparent to all intelligent observers of the English scene—all, that is, except the Covenanters. Thus the Marquis of Sabran could write in early January 1645 that there existed "little hope of moderating and making of these propositions more accommodating, and therefore I hold peace impossible." [21] Yet at this very time the Covenanters inexplicably persisted in their belief that peace would be attained. For after having constructed an unworkable treaty, they then attempted to make it succeed by granting the king concessions on a series of minor points. For example, Chancellor Loudoun tried to have Parliament acknowledge the titles of nobility recently bestowed by Charles on three of the Lords who would be negotiating at Uxbridge. He asked the Commons to yield on this issue, "lest it should make a stop in the treaty." [22]

The conduct of the Scottish commissioners in the weeks preceding Uxbridge did seem rather contradictory to contemporaries. Indeed, their paradoxical behavior led various M.P.s to become suspicious of them. As Parliament began making ready the instructions and the terms of reference for their commissioners going to Uxbridge, the Scots became increasingly more obstinate regarding the mechanics of the negotiations. The Scottish commissioners insisted that the propositions dealing with religion must be given priority over everything else; that is, before proceeding to civil matters, agreement must first be reached on a church settlement. The Commons rejected their demand, and in a debate held on January 28 and again on the 29th, members of the war party raised doubts concerning the Scots' reliability. Several militants expressed the fear that once the king acceded to Presbyterianism, the Scottish commissioners would not press him on questions vital to Parliament.[23]

The Covenanters wished religion to be the first subject on the agenda because they in turn distrusted Parliament. The Earl of Loudoun wrote Lord Warriston that if religion "were left last and civil business settled, I fear [religion] would not be stuck upon by those who would embrace peace upon any terms and with another church government than Presbyterial." [24] Both sides seemed for the moment to have lost touch with reality; for, as we have observed all along, there existed almost no likelihood that the king would accept either Presbyterianism or the civil terms of the treaty, regardless of how or in what form they were presented to him. Nevertheless, the argument over format went on until a compromise solution was at last found. The propositions would be divided into three categories: religion, the militia, and Ireland. Each would be treated for three days at a time, with religion to be discussed first. In addition, the instructions stipulated that no treaty might be signed until a satisfactory agreement had been reached on the religious proposals. The length of time for the negotiations was limited to twenty days.[25]

Considerable basis existed for the war party's suspicions of the Scots, for in actuality the latter did not feel in the least committed to Parliament's terms. In fact, during the course of the Uxbridge Treaty negotiations, Loudoun approached the Duke of Richmond and the Earl of Clarendon with the offer "that if the King should satisfy them in the business of the church, they would not concern themselves in any of the other demands." [26] That the Scots could make such a proposal demonstrates what a long distance they had traveled since the previous year. In 1643 the Covenanters had feared the consequences of a Royalist victory; now the reverse prospect frightened them. Moreover, a year's experience with English politics had left them exhausted, disillusioned, and looking for a way out. The winter of 1644-1645 represented a watershed in the war. If peace could now be settled, then Scotland would be fairly secure from her neighbor. With king and Parliament equally balanced against one another, the Scots might still act as the arbiter of English affairs. They considered that their best insurance against either a potential Laudian archbishop who might force Anglicanism down their throats, or a weak English church subverting Scotland by its sectarian example, would be a Presbyterian England. A Presbyterian church south of the border symbolized a stable future for them. "I have drawn this conclusion," wrote Sabran, "that if his Majesty slackens on religion, the Scots do not have any more demands, than those which assures their debts and secures their country." [27]

Unhappily for Scotland, their security became even more precarious than they had ever anticipated, just at the time when they could least afford it. The chief menace to the Covenanters in their homeland, the Marquis of Montrose, was busy again, and had recently been having phenomenal success in the Highlands. After his capture of Perth and Aberdeen against overwhelming odds, he invaded the Marquis of Argyll's own territory, destroying property and livestock in his wake. Even the powerful Argyll could do nothing to prevent the marauding on his own estates. On February 2, 1645 Montrose added the smashing triumph at Inverlochy to his long list of military achievements. This last defeat was an unexpected setback for the Scottish Covenanters, and a great blow to their self-assurance as well. In addition to posing a serious military problem, it served to weaken their standing in the eyes of their English allies at a crucial moment;[28] while for the king, Montrose's conquests provided an enormous boost to Royalist morale.

The battle of Inverlochy followed immediately on the arrival of the commissioners at Uxbridge on January 29. Because the two events coincided so closely, the Scottish commissioners erroneously attributed the failure of the conference to Montrose's outstanding victory. "It lost the opportunity at Uxbridge," wrote Bishop Burnet years later. And even the knowledgeable Loudoun could write at the time, "The news of Montrose's success in Scotland hath been no furtherance to our agreement."[29] Apparently the Scots had once again overestimated their own importance. In actual fact, Charles did not receive the news from Inverlochy until February 19, and by that late date the negotiations had just about run their futile course.[30]

In more ways than one, the treaty was doomed from the start. On January 30 the sessions got off to a poor beginning, when a Presbyterian minister named Christopher Love preached a violent sermon at Uxbridge, attacking the attempt to make peace at this time. In non-too-subtle language, Dr. Love told his audience, "I do not prefer a wicked peace before a just war." And after implying that the difference between Parliament and the Royalists coincided with that between heaven and hell, he went on to advise: "Deceive not yourselves, there is little likelihood of peace with such."[31] The Royalists who happened to be present during the sermon complained bitterly about it. But the king must have drawn a valuable lesson from the whole incident. For here was a Presbyterian minister vehemently opposing the peace treaty. If other Presbyterians possessed as little sympathy for Charles and his interests, what purpose could possibly be served by his acceptance of a Presbyterian church, as the Scots urged?

During the negotiations themselves, the Scottish commissioners played an active role in all the discussions. Even though Parliament included many prominent members (Holles, Whitelock, Crew, Prideaux, Pierrepoint, St. John, and Vane) in their delegation, the Scots tended to dominate the proceedings. Vane, St. John, and Prideaux, obviously opposed to any settlement, remained in the background, wisely allowing the Scots to receive the full brunt of the king's obduracy.[32]

The Scots sent to Uxbridge their most eminent churchman, Alexander Henderson, and he eloquently put forward the Scottish view. But before he proceeded very far, it became evident that Charles would not consent to an alteration in what he regarded as the only true religion of England. When Henderson confidently informed the king's delegates that Presbyterianism approximated *jure divino,* the Royalist divines replied that he was obviously mistaken, for episcopacy was the only religion which followed divine law.[33] These early encounters should have warned the Scots that there would be no compromise on religion. In fact, the king had instructed his Commissioners in advance not to accept any significant modifications in the Anglican church. Charles's stand on religion never changed. He considered government by bishops to be justified by Scripture, and necessary for his sovereignty. In a letter written at the time of the Uxbridge Treaty he observed:

> As the King's duty is to protect the church, so it is the church's to assist the King in the maintenance of his just authority; wherefore my predecessors have been always careful (and especially since the Reformation) to keep the dependency of the clergy entirely upon the Crown; without which it will scarcely sit fast upon the King's head; therefore you must do nothing to change or lessen the necessary dependency.[34]

With no progress whatsoever being made on settling the church, the negotiators moved on to the question of the militia. But here too the king's commissioners proved unyielding. To make matters worse, the Royalists went out of their way to be deliberately offensive to the Scots. Clarendon and his associates proposed that the militia should be placed in the hands of twenty persons, ten nominated by the king and ten by Parliament. When three years had elapsed, the militia would revert to its ancient condition; i.e., it would be placed under the control of the king. Furthermore, although the Parliamentary proposal on the militia included stipulations concerning the Scottish army, the Royalists refused even to acknowledge the existence of Scottish needs. As Whitelock later explained, this slight meant that

> the Scottish Commissioners were much unsatisfied that no answer was given touching the settlement of the militia in Scotland, and took it as an high neglect of that Kingdom.[35]

By the time the negotiators turned to Ireland, the Scots had assumed a most aggressive posture. They regarded Ireland as a special province of theirs, and this became clear as the sessions moved on. Along with their Parliamentary partners, the Scottish representatives condemned the cessation in Ireland; but the Scots put forth further demands. They insisted that Scotland retained a particular interest in Ireland, especially since Scottish troops were engaged in a joint Anglo-Scottish effort there, and because a Scottish general commanded the war against the Irish. The king's advisers drew rather cynical conclusions from these arguments. "The Scots Commissioners," wrote Secretary of State Edward Nicholas,

> were very eager against the cessation made in Ireland as being very prejudicial to their wicked designs to gain an interest to themselves and their nation in the government of that Kingdom.[36]

George Digby saw Ireland becoming a Scottish sphere of influence:

> For in this treaty a clear discovery is made that Ireland is wholly given to them [the Scots] by the close Committee of State.[37]

Predictably, Charles and his commissioners refused to accept the Scottish and Parliamentary terms for Ireland, insisting for their part that only the king had power to bring about a cessation.[38]

The intransigence displayed by the Scots at Uxbridge pertaining to Ireland and the militia reveals how secular issues concerned them almost as much as the religious one. While historians and even some contemporaries stress the key significance to the Covenanters of religion, it is an oversimplification to suggest that they ignored everything else. Some of the hardest negotiations took place over settling the militia question and devising the future of Ireland.

After the sessions had gone on for the allotted time of twenty days, the Royalist commissioners asked for an extension. They made their request even though no agreements had been reached in any of the three areas under discussion. The House of Lords concurred with them, and expressed the opinion that it would be worthwhile for the commissioners to stay on at Uxbridge, just in case Charles should suddenly present a new offer.[39] Perhaps the Lords had in mind the rumor then circulating that the king might decide to come to London. They knew that if he ever did appear at Westminster, popular sentiment would be won over to him, and Parliament would be forced to moderate their proposals.

The desire to continue the dialogue at Uxbridge received the support of the peace party in Commons, who took the position that any opportunity for ending the war must be pursued. Whitelock, for instance, believed that the ending of negotiations "caused much trouble in the minds of many honest men, lovers of their country's peace."[40] Nevertheless, no one could actually demonstrate how anything concrete would result from an extension. Nor were there any indications that Charles might substantially change his mind during the next few days, or even during the next few months. As a result, the Commons refused to lengthen their commissioners' mandate, thereby bringing to a close the fruitless Treaty of Uxbridge.

Despite the fact that the peace group wished to continue negotiations, the Scottish commissioners joined with the war party in arguing that nothing positive could be gained by staying on at Uxbridge. In a letter summarizing the events of the past twenty days, they wrote:

> The treaty hath not had the success we did desire and endeavor, but upon Saturday at night broke off, and yesterday we returned hither to London. That which did stick most with the King's Commissioners, and wherein was the widest difference between us, was the matter of religion. Yet no satisfaction hath been given in the other two concerning the militia and Ireland; for that the treaty did break off.[41]

Thus when Whitelock, Holles, and others called for an extension, the Scots dissented and made their views known. "There are some notions of renewing thereof [the treaty] amongst those that are most inclinable to peace," they observed, "but the time is not yet thought seasonable."[42] Loudoun, in another message sent to Scotland, expressed serious doubts concerning the king's good faith at Uxbridge. The Scottish chancellor perceived how the treaty had been initiated by Charles solely for the purpose of causing dissension within Parliament. "That which was chiefly intended by those who did treat for the King was to make objections and cast in questions to divide the two Kingdoms," he concluded.[43]

Though the Scots blamed Charles for his insincerity, the king's councillors tended to take the opposite point of view. They believed that a large share of the responsibility for the failure at Uxbridge rested with the Scots. In several Royalist accounts of the negotiations we find the theme of Scottish culpability repeated. Secretary Nicholas expressed this view in a letter to the Earl of Ormonde. "The breaking up of the treaty," he explained, "we owe (besides other good terms) to our brethren the Scots, with whom we could get no reasons to prevail."[44] The Earl of Clarendon, however, in his perceptive way realized that the Scots had merely been pawns in an elaborate game of chess played by the war party; and he saw how the leaders among the "violent spirits" encouraged the Scots to construct an unworkable treaty. Moreover, he understood how these militants, desiring a negative outcome,

> being satisfied that in the particular which concerned the church the Scots would never depart from a tittle, [were] as sure that the King would never yield to it.[45]

When the treaty, which had been intended to fail, did in fact achieve that end, the war party used the inevitable disappointment of the aftermath to suit their further designs. The road to peace appeared closed, and there remained only one alternative: the vigorous prosecution of the war. This conclusion seemed to be inescapable, and almost all factions (with the exception of the peace group) drew it. *Mercurius Britanicus* editorialized:

> Now farewell all treating forever; for we have been so often caught with that bait, that I dare say we shall swallow it no more. I hope, then, I need not tell the well affected of this Kingdom what is to be done.[46]

The moderate *Mercurius Civicus,* usually concerned with city affairs, picked up the rhetorical query and carried it one step further:

> It will now concern all of ability either by person or purse to set their helping hands to the more lively prosecution of the present war against the common enemy.[47]

The Scots, who just a short time before had been pressing for peace, now joined those voices advocating a stepping up of the war. The complete and utter rejection of Presbyterianism, combined with the rude treatment they had received at the hands of the Royalists, caused the Scots to come away from Uxbridge breathing fire. For the first time since September Scottish views coincided with those of the war party, the two groups seeing a militant solution as the only possibility. "Till both Kingdoms be in a right posture for war," Loudoun commented immediately after Uxbridge,

> it is not to be expected we shall obtain a happy and well grounded peace; therefore our next care here is to use all possible speed to strengthen our armies, remove differences betwixt the Houses and members of Parliament; that being united amongst ourselves, all may go on the more cheerfully and unanimously for carrying on of the course wherein God intends.[48]

A month later these same sentiments came echoing back from Edinburgh: ". . . the active carrying on of the war, . . . since the disappointment of our hopes in the late treaty, seems to be the only means left us for the present."[49]

When several of the Parliamentary commissioners went to Guild Hall on March 4 to explain to the city why the treaty had not succeeded, the

Scottish chancellor accompanied them. The meeting was designed for the purpose of establishing that Charles opposed a peaceful settlement, thereby leaving Parliament with no choice but to continue the war. After blaming the king for the poor results, Sir Henry Vane, Jr., one of the speakers on that day, concluded: "The only means left them [Parliament] is by a vigorous prosecution of the war."[50] This sentiment received warm endorsement from Loudoun. No one, he told his listeners, supported the treaty more "than myself and my fellow Commissioners for the Kingdom of Scotland." But he soon learned that

> so prevalent with his Majesty were the councils of those who labor to subvert religion and introduce an arbitrary and tyrannical power, that our propositions for religion were altogether rejected.

Therefore,

> it was then high time for the watchmen to give the alarm to the people, and warn them of their danger, lest they should be deceived with the vain hopes of peace.[51]

Both Loudoun and Vane then asked the city to contribute the necessary funds for putting a vigorous army in the field.

As events demonstrated, the failure of the Uxbridge Treaty furthered the goals of the war party. Even while the sessions were going on, news filtered back to London of the improbability of any agreement, and this information enabled the war forces to press on with their aims. Accordingly, on February 15 the Lords finally withdrew their objections to the ordinance for the remodeling of the army, and the measure became law.[52] Ten days later the House of Commons revived the committee that had drafted the original Self-Denying Ordinance, for the purpose of producing a second one. This time, however, instead of turning the committee over to moderates, the Commons named William Ellis, a war-party adherent, as chairman.[53]

The militants also managed to provide Sir Thomas Fairfax with a free hand in nominating his subordinates. Though the peace party objected to a few of his selections (e.g., Colonel Rich and Captain Boughe), none of the men chosen seems to have been excluded. The Lords, however, endeavored to weed out a large number of senior officers, and they rejected Colonels Pickering and Montague as well as about forty captains.[54] On this occasion the upper house had the backing of the Scots, who expressed dissatisfaction at the large number of Independents being given command in the New Model. On March 4 John Glyn brought in a paper from the Scottish commissioners requesting that Parliament "would be careful to name officers well affected to the uniformity of church government." They also desired that Parliament "would constitute experienced soldiers to be commanders."[55] (Read "Scottish officers" for "experienced soldiers.") Three leading members of the war party, Vane, Prideaux, and Strode, took immediate offense, and proceeded to attack the paper as a breach of Parliamentary privilege. They based their argument on the fact that the list of commanders had already been sent up to the House of Lords. John Glyn, Denzil Holles, and Sir Philip Stapleton tried to smooth over the incident, but it was obvious that the Scots had sent their letter too late, and had been tactless besides. Because it was written after the list had been drawn up, their petition carried little weight, and had no appreciable effect on the outcome.[56]

The Lords, meanwhile, continued to withhold their approval from the forty-odd officers, even though the Commons repeatedly pressed them to give their assent. Those in favor of the original list pointed out that the delay in selecting officers prevented the New Model Army from being formed—a serious handicap, since the Royalist forces had already taken the field.[57] On March 17 a division held in the Lords, on the issue of letting Fairfax's list go through, resulted in a tie vote of ten for each side. Lord Say produced a proxy vote belonging to Lord Mulgrave, who supported the original names. The vote carried next day, with the upper house approving the new officers without any substitutions or omissions.[58] According to Edward Bowles, the minister, it was the city which in the end forced the Lords to assent. They had presented a petition declaring "their willingness to bring in money in case the list passed."[59]

The passing of the New Model Ordinance in its final form came as a great blow to the Scots. Over 300 Scottish officers who formerly served with

Parliament were retired, and this number included Manchester's aide, General Crawford. Their replacements were Englishmen, including several Independents, though not quite as many as the Scots imagined. As the Marquis de Sabran pointed out, this elimination of their countrymen considerably reduced the Scottish role in English affairs, as well as the Scots' importance in the eyes of the English.[60]

While Parliament placed the finishing touches on the new army, the nagging and unresolved issue of the Self-Denying Ordinance continued to divide the two houses. On March 24, after going on record with lavish praise for the faithfulness of the Lords as well as for their Lordships' "unwearied endeavors for the public good," the Commons passed the revised version of the ordinance for the first and second times.[61] The measure, as ratified by the lower house a week later, differed somewhat from the December 9 version. The most significant addition was a clause which specified that members of Parliament who held offices had forty days in which to surrender their posts. Once the principle of a period of grace had been introduced, these forty days could be extended in special circumstances.

The Lords put up a feeble resistance to the new ordinance, but as Essex and Manchester had in effect lost their armies, there seemed no point in trying to withstand the strong line taken by the Commons. The Earl of Essex was encouraged by members of the peace party to refuse to resign his position, but at this late stage any further resistance on his part would have had little more than nuisance value. Moreover, it might serve to divide Parliament just when their new army took the field for the first time. On April 2 the loyal Essex gave up the ghost by resigning his commission, followed immediately by the Earl of Manchester. A day later the upper house ratified the Self-Denying Ordinance.[62] When the time came to ratify Sir Thomas Fairfax's commission, the Lords were too demoralized to resist; this despite the fact that the ordinance giving Fairfax his commission failed to include the usual clause concerning the preservation of the king's person.[63]

With this body of legislation behind them, Parliament could finally turn the war over to the generals. Those members of the Commons who had seen the New Model Ordinance through all its stages felt confident that the new army would bring victory. Nevertheless, the success which would come to the New Model remained, at this stage, far from a certainty. A few months at the minimum were needed to convert the old military establishment into a viable force. Indeed, many believed that the overhauling of the army served to weaken Parliament's condition. The Royalists, for example, displayed little regard for the new force, expressing their contempt quite openly. In Oxford the New Model Army was referred to derisively as the "new noodle."[64] The king himself believed that his relative standing in relation to Parliament had definitely improved. He expressed his optimism to Henrietta Maria on March 27, 1645:

> The general face of my affairs me thinks to mend; the dissensions at London rather increasing than ceasing, Montrose daily prospering, my western business mending apace, and hopeful in all the rest. So that if I had reasonable supplies of money and powder (not to exclude any other) I am confident to be in a better condition this year, than I have been since this rebellion began.[65]

NOTES

1. Meikle, p. 53.
2. *Scottish Dove,* February 7, 1645, wrote cautiously concerning the New Model Ordinance: "Necessity requires a change, though with some dangers or prejudices."
3. C.S.P. Ven., p. 172.
4. C.J., III, p. 684.
5. Whitelock, II, p. 327. It is interesting to note that Whitelock and Glyn, both affiliated with the peace group, were certainly not *jure divino* Presbyterians; most likely they were Erastians.
6. *Acts and Ordinances,* I, pp. 582-607.
7. C.J., III, p. 733.
8. Ibid., IV, pp. 20, 28.

9. To be exact, the king would be asked to approve of "the Covenant, the Directory for Worship, the votes given in by the Assembly of Divines concerning church government and passed the houses; the assenting to the bill against Episcopacy and the ratifying and ordinance for the calling of the Assembly of Divines" (ibid., pp. 35-36).
10. See, for example, S. R. Gardiner, *Civil War,* II, p. 110.
11. Baillie, II, p. 250.
12. Hugh Trevor-Roper, *Archbishop Laud* (London, 1962), p. 422.
13. Sabran, S P O/31/3/75, fol. 166v.
14. *Acts and Ordinances,* I, p. 608.
15. *Mercurius Aulicus,* January 11, 1645.
16. Peter Heylyn, *The History of the Presbyterians* (Oxford, 1670), p. 468.
17. Clarendon, III, p. 465.
18. See chap. II, above.
19. *Constitutional Documents,* pp. 282-283.
20. L.J., VII, p. 219.
21. Sabran, 5461, fol. 22v.
22. Whitacre, fol. 377.
23. Wodrow MSS, National Library of Scotland, Edinburgh, LXVII, fol. 28.
24. Ibid. Among other things, this quote indicates that the Scots were not working in alliance with the peace group at this time.
25. C.J., IV, pp. 35-36.
26. Clarendon, III, pp. 476-477. Clarendon, however, gave the Scots no encouragement.
27. Sabran, S P O/31/3/76, fol. 76v.
28. Curiously, the reaction of the Scottish commissioners to Montrose's victories was one of embarrassment rather than of animosity toward the king (Sabran, 5461, fol. 65v).
29. Gilbert Burnet, *History of His Own Time,* 2 vols. (London, 1724), I, p. 40; Wodrow MSS, LXVII, fol. 32.
30. *The King's Cabinet,* T.T., E. 292 (27).
31. T.T., E. 274 (15).
32. Clarendon, III, p. 492.

33. Whitelock, II, pp. 378-379.
34. T.T., E. 292 (27).
35. Whitelock, II, p. 385.
36. Thomas Carte (ed.), *A Collection of Letters Written by Charles I,* 3 vols. (London, 1735), I, pp. 393-394.
37. Ibid., pp. 383-384.
38. Whitelock, II, p. 387.
39. L.J., VII, p. 203.
40. Whitelock, II, p. 395. "Honest Men" should be read "members of the peace group."
41. Meikle, pp. 60-61.
42. Ibid., pp. 62-63.
43. Wodrow MSS, LXVII, fol. 32.
44. Carte, op. cit., p. 392.
45. Clarendon, III, p. 493.
46. *Mercurius Britanicus,* March 3, 1645.
47. *Mercurius Civicus,* February 27, 1645.
48. Wodrow MSS, LXVII, fol. 32.
49. C.S.P.D., 1644-45, p. 392.
50. T.T., E. 273 (3).
51. Ibid.
52. L.J., VII, p. 195. An added incentive was the recent mutiny in Waller's army.
53. C.J., IV, p. 62.
54. Whitacre, fol. 396.
55. Dewes, 166, fol. 181b. The Scottish note was delivered on March 4, 1945.
56. Ibid. See below, chap. V, for the political significance of this episode.
57. Whitacre, fol. 396.
58. Ibid., fol. 397. The Earl of Essex, in turn, produced a proxy vote from his brother-in-law, the Earl of St. Albans, but this was disallowed on the grounds that St. Albans was a Catholic.
59. Letter from Edward Bowles to Lord Fairfax, March 18, 1645, in Robert Bell (ed.), *The Correspondence of the Fairfax Family* (London, 1849), p. 168.

60. Sabran, 5461, fol. 175v.
61. C.J., IV, p. 88.
62. Ibid., pp. 96-97; Whitelock, II, p. 415.
63. L.J., VII, p. 298.
64. Whitelock, II, p. 415.
65. T.T., E. 292 (27).

V

"A Lame Erastian Presbytery"

As the focus of events shifted from the conference table to the battlefield, the Covenanters stood to profit. At the time of the Uxbridge Treaty their prestige had fallen, mainly because the Scottish army had contributed little to the Parliamentary cause since the summer of 1644. But with the resumption of the spring campaign of 1645 it became apparent that the Covenanters still had an important role to play in the war. The New Model Army, as yet an unknown and untried quantity, required auxiliary support from them. Thus, when the Committee of Both Kingdoms on January 30 recommended to the Commons that the Scottish army be summoned southward to protect the midlands, it was Cromwell who personally made the request.[1]

The Scots commissioners in England appreciated Parliament's need for military aid from Scotland. "That the condition of affairs is such here, as without the speedy assistance by your army you may have this Kingdom for lost," one of them reported to Edinburgh on February 18.[2] Their underlining of Parliament's request for help was, of course, nothing new;

throughout the war the commissioners had been urging their army on to greater efforts. When Parliament requested the Scottish army to march south, they sent a special note of their own to General Leven, impressing upon him the importance of carrying out the order.[3]

The Earl of Leven would very much have liked to comply with the directive to move south, but for the present he found himself unable to do so. His army remained undersupplied, underpaid, and financially indebted to the northern counties it now occupied, with no relief apparently forthcoming. Until some remedy could be found for this dilemma, the Scottish army intended to stay put.

The growing vulnerability of his homeland added to Leven's problems, for haunting Scotland at that very moment was the specter of Montrose. The latter, with his band of "Irish rebels and malignants," freely roamed the Highlands, notching up a series of impressive victories and posing a rather serious threat to the Covenanters. With Montrose at his rear, the Earl of Leven had to give second thoughts to a southern campaign in England that took his army increasingly further away from Scotland. Each day's march would have to be retraced in the event of a summons from Edinburgh.[4]

The English Parliament assumed a curious attitude toward the threat posed to Scotland by Montrose: they behaved as if no danger existed. Members of Parliament evidently believed that the Scots had been brought into the war for the sole purpose of helping Parliament, and not for the latter to worry about their northern ally. One receives the distinct impression that few in London cared to be bothered about Scotland; if the Scots had difficulties, that was certainly unfortunate, but their troubles would have to remain their own affair. Even as conditions deteriorated, Parliament never accepted the presence of Montrose as a legitimate excuse for the inaction of the Scottish army in England.

Making believe that Montrose did not exixt was one matter, but inducing the Scots to march south became quite another. For an army needs supplies before it can fight, and this simple fact an unsympathetic Parliament was forced to recognize. In order to get the Scottish army moving, the House of Commons on February 18 offered to provide Leven with £31,000 per month, a sum which the House of Lords felt obliged to cut by £10,000.[5]

These offers of funds, especially the last from the Lords, did not greatly encourage the Covenanters. According to the treaty of November 1643 they were entitled to £31,000 per month, whereas the total stipulated by the Lords, later confirmed by the Commons, reduced their proposed income by one-third. But in February 1645 the amount promised seemed irrelevant, as the Scots had rarely been paid at all since their entry into the war. In 1643 Parliament had hoped to obtain the money to pay the Scots from confiscated estates of Royalists and Catholics, but these seizures were never adequate to provide regular payment. Another potential source of income, the receipts from Newcastle coal, also proved disappointing.[6] Now, in February, 1645, Parliament held out the additional assurances of greater regularity of payment to impress their Scottish allies. The funds would come from taxes levied on the southern counties and the city of London, the latter to be the main supplier.[7] But promises had been made before and then broken; it would take more than words to move Leven and his troops. For the time being, then, the impoverished Scottish army remained immobile in the north of England.

However valid their complaints of inadequate supplies may have been, the Scots received very little sympathy from Parliament. During a debate on February 27 concerning the manner of payment to the Scots army, a few members of the Commons actually suggested that the first £21,000 (still not raised) should be sent only part of the way to Newcastle. In other words, if they wanted money, they would have to move southward to receive it. A suggestion of this sort indicates the lack of consideration now openly expressed about Scottish needs. Fortunately tact won out on this occasion, and the proposal was abandoned on the grounds that the Covenanters might receive the impression that their English allies did not trust them.[8]

The debate regarding the manner in which the Scots would be paid proved to be purely academic. For during the next few months they continued to receive just what they had been getting all along from London: very little.[9] And although they provided hardly any financial support for the Scots, the two houses kept insisting that the Covenanters come south. On April 4 the Commons desired the Committee of Both Kingdoms to "earnestly press the Scots Commissioners, that their army may speedily advance." Ten days later a similar message from the lower house arrived at the joint committee requesting it "to earnestly move the Commissioners of the Kingdom of Scotland to give present order to hasten the advancement of that commanded party of the Scots army." [10] On one of these occasions in April when the English members called on the Scots commissioners to get their sluggish army on the move, the Scots attempted a defense of their countrymen. Whereupon Sir Henry Vane, Jr., castigated them with the charge that their troops had "poorly contributed to the war and to the service of Parliament, while having drawn much money." He concluded his charge with the cutting remark that the Scots looked out only for their own interests, and had little concern for the fate of England.[11]

By the spring of 1645 the reputation of the Covenanters in the eyes of their allies, as Robert Baillie observed, "hath been much lower than before." Baillie went on to enumerate the reasons for this decline:

> The lasting troubles which a handful of Irish [i.e., Montrose] hath brought upon our whole land was the beginning of our disgrace. The much talked of weakness of our army in England did add unto it. Our necessity to lie upon the northern shires, almost exhausted by the King's army before and their daily outcries of our oppression, made it to increase. But that which highly advanced it is our delay to march southward, after all their importune calls. These things have made us here almost contemptible.[12]

Understandably the Scots grew alarmed at their growing unpopularity. To help offset the criticism directed at them, and to strengthen their own hand in English affairs, the Scottish commissioners decided to end their policy of nonalignment in Parliamentary politics. Their experience with the war party had made them chary of any political commitments in London, though on a few occasions in the recent past the commissioners had worked with the peace group. Yet until they encountered open hostility, the Scots had generally preferred to remain unencumbered by an alliance.[13]

The first indication that the Scots commissioners had joined forces with the peace party on a more permanent basis appeared in a letter which *Mercurius Aulicus* printed on February 27, 1645. This letter, intercepted by the Royalists, had been sent by John Pyne, member of Parliament from

Poole, to his cousin, Colonel Popham. The Royalists presumably published it to embarrass both Parliament and the Scots. In his missive,[14] Pyne described how the Scottish commissioners had broken away from those who controlled the Committee of Both Kingdoms (specifically, Vane, St. John, Cromwell, Haselrig, Crew, Wallop, and Pierrepoint) and "have joined themselves in a seeming confederacy and compliance with Sir Philip Stapleton and his associates: viz., Holles, the Recorder, Clotworthy, Reynolds, Whitelock, Maynard and the Lords."[15] As a "violent" himself, Pyne seemed dubious that such a *volte face* by the Scots and the peace party could be permanent. "Yet I cannot think them [the Scots] such fools," he added, "as to trust and deliver themselves over unto the designs and stratagems of those that they know do hate them, and are their enemies in heart."[16]

John Pyne, who evidently looked for consistency in politics, found it extremely difficult to understand how the former opponents and chief critics of the Scots could become their allies. However, for the Scots, presumably in England to accomplish a great Christian mission, the explanation appeared simple. In their semiofficial presentation of events, David Buchanan's *Truth Its Manifest,* the Scots described the shift in alliances as merely a rectification of a previous oversight, the oversight having been made by the peace group. According to this version, those who had opposed the Scottish entry into the war and had tried to hinder them at every possible opportunity suddenly discovered that they had been wrong in their estimation of the Scots. "Now at last," wrote Buchanan about the peace party,

> bethinking themselves of their own errors and how that, without reason, they had been jealous of the Scots, they began to go along with them more freely and earnestly in the public work than they had done heretofore; which the Scots, minding mainly the furthering of the service of the common cause, take kindly at their hands, and welcome the expressions of their good affection to the service, with respective civility.[17]

It would be unrealistic to expect Buchanan to be completely objective in a tract designed to present the Scottish viewpoint. Yet his account is the opposite of the truth. In reality it was the peace group who, far from converting to a Scottish position in politics, had in fact maintained a steady course throughout the Civil War. They continued to work for a negotiated settlement at every opportunity, as they had done since the conflict began. The Scots, on the other hand, because of their original connection with the militants, had frequently supported war-party policies. Even after the break with St. John and Vane in September 1644, the Scots occasionally found themselves on the same side of an issue as the war party, most recently on the decision to end negotiations at Uxbridge.

For a more accurate description of how the new alliance became established, one can turn to the *Memoirs of Denzil Holles,* a source which must, admittedly, be used with care. But in regard to the conduct of the Scots during their first years of involvement in the war, Holles did draw some perceptive conclusions. For example, he realized that they had been disoriented in their first contact with English politicians, thereby providing easy pickings for the war party. But after their initial confusion, the Scots

> found that the other party [the peace group] had been misrepresented, being the men who, in truth, did agree with them in principle and in design: which was only to reform, not to alter, to regulate and so to save, not to destroy.[18]

The alliance between the peace party and the Scots first manifested itself when Parliament began selecting new officers for the New Model Army.[19] During this process the Commons, as we saw, systematically excluded Scottish officers from positions of command. Realizing belatedly how the creation of the new army weakened them, the Scots decided to make their displeasure known. On March 4, 1645 they requested the House of Commons to ensure that only those willing to take the Covenant and who "were well affected to the uniformity of church government" be made officers. They further requested that Parliament do its best to see that "experienced soldiers be named commanders in the new army."[20] Both these demands, if accepted, would keep the Scottish officers employed in England. But the Commons rejected the Scots' petition out of hand, even implying that it could be interpreted as a breach of Parliamentary privilege.[21]

Whether the Scots might have succeeded in preventing the mass dismissal of Scottish officers if they had acted earlier is debatable, but it was certain after the rejection of their petition that nothing more could be done. In terms of concrete results their effort had failed; nevertheless, the incident marked a significant development. For when the Scots commissioners presented their petition to the Commons they received the active support of the peace party.[22] This was the first time that Holles, Stapleton, and their associates had come out so unreservedly and strongly for the Scots on a major issue in Parliament. In December 1644 the cooperation between the two groups regarding the removal of Cromwell had of necessity been furtive, and it had been ephemeral as well. Now, in March 1645, an open and lasting alliance had been formed, one that was destined to endure for the remainder of the first Civil War.

When previously the war party allied themselves with the Scots, they managed to exploit the association for their own ends. Frequently they used Scottish backing to push through legislation in Parliament that might not have passed otherwise. The Scots, in turn, benefited from the relationship up to a certain point. But that point was a crucial one indeed, for it concerned the nature of the future religious settlement. On this rock the alliance foundered, never again to be restored. Approximately one-half year after the militants abandoned the Covenanters, the peace group decided to join forces with them. The delay in cementing the new bonds, we can be sure, indicated that the decision had not been a precipitous one. Potential sources of friction existed and had to be overcome. Yet both parties felt that their working together at this time was important enough for them to overlook their various differences.

For the peace party the added prestige of Scottish support would, it was hoped, serve to provide a needed fillip at a time when the militants seemed to be dominating Parliament. The leadership of the peace group apparently believed that they could capitalize on the Scots in the same way that the war party had done in the past, thus reversing the increasingly militant trend which characterized Parliament in the winter of 1644-1645. The Covenanters welcomed the new alliance as an excellent chance to stem the recent decline of their position in England, and even to strengthen their hand. Being without an ally for six months had proven nearly disastrous for them; they sorely needed spokesmen to defend their interests in Parliament, and the peace party were prepared to do just this. Therefore, for extremely practical reasons the Scots in 1645 were willing to link their fate with the party they had so energetically opposed in the past.

The Scots, one would think, had rendered a coalition more difficult during the previous months when they began viewing the Civil War increasingly in religious terms. At Uxbridge, for instance, the Earl of Loudoun had informed Clarendon that his countrymen would use their influence to moderate Parliament's peace terms if the king promised to accept Presbyterianism.[23] Again, toward the latter part of March the French resident, Sabran, communicated the distinct impression that the Scots' sole interest in the Civil War was to see England a Presbyterian country. "On religion all depends," the Scots commissioners had told Sabran.[24] Such was the state of affairs that the Scots even tried to convince themselves that the English Parliament had gone to war with the king mainly for the purpose of a "true reformation of religion."[25] With this growing emphasis on the religious character of their role, how could the Presbyterian Scots form an alliance with a party whose leading members were themselves anti-Presbyterian?[26]

Politics, it has frequently been observed, is the art of the possible; and practitioners of this art, if they are successful, manage to find ways of reconciling seemingly irreconcilable differences. The alliance between the Scots and the peace party became a classic example of a *mariage de convenance.* Political arrangements of this nature have, in the main, a tendency to be rather ephemeral. The alliance between the Scots and the peace group, however, proved to be extremely durable. An important reason for its success was the fact that each of the two parties knew precisely where the other stood on the major issues of the day. In contrast to their first alliance with the militants, the Scots entered this association with their eyes open.

One reason for the customary failure of marriages of convenience is that they tend to involve compromises which are difficult to maintain for any length of time. The Scots/peace party alliance entailed a compromise which demanded such sacrifices on the part of the Scots that one could never have imagined that they would be willing to accept its terms. The Covenanters, who entered the Civil War for a multitude of reasons, began, as we saw, to subordinate everything to religion. Their new allies, for the most part, had no absolute commitment to ideals, certainly not to a religious one. Men like Holles, Stapleton, and Maynard were practical politicians who, though they may have held strong principles, wished to effectuate the best settlement under existing circumstances. Therefore, it might have been predicted that for any alliance between the peace group and the Scots to work, the former would surely accept the Scottish position on religion. In return, the Scots would presumably lend their support to moderate proposals for peace. But in fact this quid pro quo did not materialize. While the Scots accepted the peace group's formula for ending the war, it appears that the latter never promised to work for the establishment of an orthodox Presbyterian church.[27] As will be seen, necessity compelled the Scots to be satisfied with the Erastian form of Presbyterianism—a religious settlement which most nearly met the specifications of the membership of the peace party, and which had always been anathema to the Scots.

The nature of the compromise made by the Scots did not immediately become evident. Indeed, some of the Scottish divines seem to have been sheltered from the realities of the alliance, and continued to believe that a pure form of Presbyterianism could be achieved in England, despite the fact that no such commitment had ever been made by the peace-party leadership. Months previously the Scots had begun referring to their political opponents in England as the "Independents."[28] Since their chief opposition within the Westminster Assembly had in truth come from the religious Independents, they considered it logical to describe the militants in this manner, while labeling their political allies, the "Presbyterians." These religious designations caught on and became commonly used to differentiate the two most active parties in Parliament, resulting in a general confusion.

From 1645 onward, one finds the terms "Independent" and "Presbyterian" used to distinguish the two leading factions with greater and greater frequency. Before long these religious designations for political parties became common parlance, to be employed not only by the Scots but by all the other political participants as well. The fact that contemporaries divided parties in this manner has naturally led historians to do the same thing; for historians tend to assume that contemporaries know what they are talking about. In most instances this is a correct assumption, but unfortunately in this case it is not. Indeed, it would be very difficult to find terms more inaccurate to delimit members of Parliament in the 1640s than "Presbyterian" and "Independent." [29]

The leaders of the peace party at the time of their alliance with the Scots were, as we have just seen, definitely not Presbyterians in religion. By the same token, it has been convincingly demonstrated that few members of the war party adhered to Independency.[30] As Professor J. H. Hexter has shown, more "Independents" associated themselves with the presbyteries established as part of the Presbyterian settlement than did "Presbyterians," indicating that a great many political "Independents" held rather flexible views.[31]

In reality the vast majority of members of the Long Parliament were neither Presbyterian nor Independent, but Erastian. Contemporaries grasped this fact in their more lucid moments. Thus, for example, Robert Baillie, who frequently threw the terms "Presbyterian" and "Independent" around loosely, and therefore bears a great responsibility for the confusion, knew this to be the case. "The most of the House of Commons are downright Erastians," he wrote on April 25, 1645. "They are like to create us much more woe than all the sectaries of England." [32]

No Erastian party existed in the formal sense, nor did it function as a coherent body in the manner in which, for example, both the war and peace groups did. What Baillie meant when he spoke of the Erastianism of the Long Parliament was the anticlerical sentiment then prevailing: a distrust of a church independent of Parliamentary control. The experience with Archbishop Laud had left the members suspicious of autonomous church officials wielding great arbitrary power. Consequently, a Presbyterian church resembling the Scottish model would be just as distasteful to a majority in Parliament as was the Anglicanism of Charles I and Laud. Milton did not speak for himself alone when he remarked that a new presbyter would be but an old priest writ large.

The incident in 1645 involving Thomas Coleman confirmed the picture drawn by Baillie. On July 30, 1645 the House of Commons arranged to have Coleman deliver the monthly fast sermon. These monthly sermons had become a regular part of Parliamentary procedure since 1642; but Coleman had been selected at this time, as the Scots believed, to air the religious beliefs of a majority of the members. Coleman, formerly a rector in Lincolnshire and now a member of the Assembly of Divines, was a well-known Erastian, and had been encouraged to come forward as a religious spokesman for Parliament. Wrote Baillie:

> The lawyers in Parliament, making it their work to sport our Presbytery, did blow up the poor man with much vanity, so he is become their champion, to bring out, in the best way he can, Erastus' arguments against the proposition [exclusion of scandalous persons from the sacrament by the church elders] for the contentment of the Parliament.[33]

In his sermon on July 30 Coleman deprecated equally the Presbyterians and the Independents, finding fault especially with their claims of *jure divino,* "the one with a national determination, the other with a congregational engagement." His advice to the Commons: ignore the pretensions of both and "establish as few things *jure divino* as can well be." To his responsive audience, Coleman went on to warn against giving clerics control over church administration. "Lay no more burden of government upon the shoulders of ministers, than Christ plainly laid upon them," he advised. And using a comparison which later drew fire from the Presbyterians, he maintained that those clerics who desired governing authority for themselves followed the same path as the Antichrist, the pope. To ward off creeping Papism, Parliament should endeavor to keep the government of the English church in its own hands. "So say I," Coleman advised Parliament, "give us doctrine, take you government."[34]

Coleman won the applause of the Commons for his forthright sermon. In fact, so pleased was John Glyn, a leading member of the peace party, that he asked that the minister be allowed to preach again.[35] Glyn's approval confirms that the members of the peace group, far from compromising their religious views to satisfy the Scots, remained as Erastian as ever.

The rector from Lincolnshire elicited a rather different reaction from some of his fellow clerics. Indeed, Coleman and the views he expressed posed a significant threat to all Presbyterians. This fact did not go unnoticed among the Scots, who regarded the sermon as a challenge directed at themselves. It was therefore fitting that a young Scottish divine, George Gillespie, should deliver the first public rebuttal to Coleman. The most learned and articulate of all the Scottish ministers, Gillespie preached before the House of Lords on August 27, the monthly fast day. He devoted almost his entire lecture to what he euphemistically termed "a brotherly examination of some passage of Mr. Coleman's late printed sermon." Needless to say, his treatment of his fellow cleric was anything but brotherly. The Lords heard Coleman accused of being an Erastian (which he most certainly was), of working against the reformation of religion, and of violating the Solemn League and Covenant. And in one particularly sharp passage, Gillespie returned his antagonist's insult by likening Coleman, and all Erastians for that matter, to the hated Papists.[36]

In the usual manner, Gillespie received the formal appreciation of the House of Lords for his sermon; and he had produced an effective answer to the Erastian position. But in all probability he actually antagonized a great many members, for his was virtually the last invitation received by a Scotsman to preach to the Long Parliament.[37] The Erastian English Parliament obviously was not ready for conversion.

When Robert Baillie predicted that the Erastians in the Long Parliament would cause the Scots much woe, he could not have realized the extent to which his prognosis would be borne out by events. The religious settlement of 1646 confirmed the worst of his fears. This new church created by Parliament may have had the distinction of being known as "Presbyterian," but its most Presbyterian feature was its name.[38]

It has been observed by many historians[39] that English Presbyterianism was, by Scottish standards, a somewhat anemic affair. Certainly it had a distinct Erastian flavor to it. Ultimate appeal on points of controversy rested not with the ecclesiastical leaders, but with Parliament. The two houses at Westminster would become the final authority on all church matters, and any later Parliament had the freedom to make substantial alterations whenever it felt inclined to do so. The English Presbyterian church, as Robert Baillie lamented, was "a lame Erastian Presbytery."[40]

Erastian–or Parliamentary–Presbyterianism had the overwhelming support of the membership of both houses. On March 7, 1646, when one of the key planks of the new religious legislation passed the Commons, the entire lower house accompanied the ordinance to the Lords. And on this occasion a leading member of the Commons delivered a speech to the House of Lords, informing the peers that "this is the dawning of a glorious day which our ancestors hoped to have seen but could not." The man who thus praised the Erastian settlement was Denzil Holles, a leader of the English "Presbyterians."[41]

When some of the Scottish divines criticized their English brethren for establishing what they regarded as an imperfect church, they did so because they misunderstood the nature of the present conflict. That is to say, the Scots failed to understand–or perhaps they did not wish to see–that the English Civil War was essentially a political struggle. For most of the participants victory in the war took precedence over every other issue; indeed, in reality, religious preference played a secondary role to the essential matters of peace and war.

This fact can be demonstrated by the continuing affiliation of religious Presbyterians with the war party throughout 1645, at a time when the Scots were already distinguishing between "Presbyterian" and "Independent" political parties. In the eyes of the Scots, as well as of most other contemporaries, the "Independent party" succeeded what had formerly been the war party. But as we have already noted, political parties could not be characterized by religious belief. Thus a coalition of militants, religious Independents, and some religious Presbyterians still continued to operate in 1645, as it had earlier, even though the Scots tried to identify it with only one of its components, i.e., the Independents. This coalition endured as a viable force at a time when some of its members advocated a rigid Presbyterianism while others favored toleration of the sects.

Religious Presbyterians who sided with the war party in 1644 played an active role subsequently as well. William Strode, whose Presbyterianism could never be impugned, voted with the militants on political issues, even serving as a teller for the war party in two separate divisions in 1645.[42] Francis Rous and Zouch Tate were so anxious to have Scottish Presbyterianism adopted in England that they advised the Scottish divines regularly on how best to work for this goal. Yet in 1645 both aligned themselves with this coalition; and Rous, evidently the more firmly committed of the two, maintained his association with the war party ("Independents") until the

Protectorate.[43] Edmund Prideaux opposed granting toleration to "tender consciences" in September 1644, yet he voted with the war party in 1645, and in 1647 fled to the army along with other hard-core "Independents." [44] A final example might be William Ellis, a man as eager for the establishment of pure Presbyterianism as any. At one point in August 1644 he wished to expel from the Commons those M.P.s who still neglected to take the Covenant. In 1646 he became a Presbyterian elder. Nevertheless, in March of the previous year, Ellis had brought into the House of Commons the Second Self-Denying Ordinance; and when the first Protectorate Parliament met, sitting among its ranks was one William Ellis.[45]

If religious Presbyterians did indeed vote with the war party, and the leaders of the peace group remained as Erastian as the majority in Parliament, why the pretense of calling an Erastian party "Presbyterian"? The leaders of the peace group, as far as we know, raised no objections to their new name. The use of this inapplicable designation apparently soothed Scottish sensibilities and made it easier for High Presbyterians to support them; otherwise they would not have begun the fiction. Denzil Holles later confessed that he employed "Presbyterianism" to oppose "Independency"; that is, he made use of religion as a device to strengthen his party's political standing.[46]

In regard to religion, the service rendered to the Scots and the Presbyterian ministers of London by Holles and his associates was really negligible. The political "Presbyterians" could not be converted from their belief in a church dominated by Parliament to one controlled by presbyters. At most the peace party would be willing to accept Presbyterian frills on a basically Erastian church, and to satisfy the Scots they would even agree to call the new church "Presbyterian." Sir Philip Stapleton, his eulogist informs us, had little interest in changing the English church "for the Covenant and church government of presbytery"; but after the alliance with the Scots he felt that a pseudo-"Presbyterian" church settlement might make the Scots "happy." [47] In this manner, leaders of the peace group like Stapleton helped to bring about that "lame Erastian presbytery" which Parliament eventually established in 1646.

The "Presbyterian party" might take credit for Parliament's "Presbyterian" settlement, thereby strengthening the myth that they themselves were Presbyterian. But very obviously, the High Presbyterians remained dissatisfied. They could, however, do little to alter the course Parliament had taken. Presbyterian ministers, both Scottish and English, hoped that the city of London, which in 1646 seemed sympathetic to them, would fight the establishment of an Erastian church and demand a true Presbyterianism. Their hopes proved vain, however, and they were sorely disappointed when the city declined to take strong action. "The City has much grieved us," moaned Baillie in the spring of 1646, "by their unexpected fainting; they will greatly repent it, but out of time." [48]

Real Presbyterians remained dissatisfied with the nature of the church settlement, but the real Independents did not appear to be greatly disturbed. True, in the extensive religious legislation passed in 1645 and 1646 no mention was made of toleration, or of the tender feelings of tender consciences.[49] But despite this omission, the religious Independents could not have been overly disappointed. After all, their chief opponents, the real Presbyterians, had, so to speak, been disarmed by Parliament. Moreover, they realized that the creation of a hierarchical structure with Parliament at the summit permitted dissenters to appeal over the heads of the clergy; an arrangement which, because of its inherent inefficiency (i.e., the inevitable delay that appeals would entail), gave the Independents a greater measure of security. Also, since the machinery was new and cumbersome, the suppression of deviant views might prove infinitely more difficult than the Presbyterians had hoped.

Many sectaries would agree with the advice tendered by an anonymous pamphleteer, who told his fellow non-Presbyterians simply to ignore the existence of the new church government. *Several Votes of Tender Conscience,* written in May 1646, concluded with the reminder that since the Parliamentary settlement had not the benefit of God's word, those of "tender conscience and the friends thereof shall be exempt therefrom." [50]

There is reason to believe that the religious Independents in Parliament did not put up any resistance to the church settlement. Realizing that an Erastian government was the best that could be obtained, considering their own limited numbers, these Independents either gave active support, or at the least did not offer substantial opposition, to the relevant legislation. In October 1645 Sir Henry Vane, Jr., told the Scots to be satisfied with the

Presbyterian government to be established by Parliament. "The sense of the House," Vane believed, "could not admit, nor ought the Kingdom of Scotland to press," for all that the assembly desired.[51] If Vane advised the Scots to be reconciled with the new ecclesiastical structure, then surely he himself must have been so.

If the Independents or some of the more extreme sectaries still feared that there would be rigid repression of the sects, then the treatment of Paul Best must have alleviated their apprehensions. In the religiously conscious, Puritan atmosphere of London during the Civil War, Best had the temerity to deny the Holy Trinity—which was a blasphemy of the worst order. In 1645 the civil authorities imprisoned him, and on March 28, 1646 the House of Commons ordered that he be punished for his infamous views "by hanging him until he be dead." Once having ordered this the Commons drew back: some thought that Best should be given a chance to change his mind. On April 4 a committee consisting of members of the lower house and divines from the Westminster Assembly asked him to confess his errors. But Best, a man of strong ideals, refused their request outright. Back he went to his prison cell, where he compounded his crime by writing a pamphlet entitled *Mysteries Discovered,* in which he attempted to convert others. Yet inexplicably, nothing further was done to him. Finally, toward the end of 1647, Best received his release from prison. He was now free to go about his business, and presumably to express his views without further reprisals.[52] This case illustrates that English (Erastian) Presbyterianism did not seriously threaten the existence of the Independents, nor even of the sects. If a Paul Best could survive, certainly a Philip Nye and a Robert Goodwin could breathe quite easily; and so, for that matter, could any other sectary.

Thus the Independents felt secure because of the Erastianism of the new church, believing as they did that it protected them against strict enforcement of Presbyterian orthodoxy. Yet it should be pointed out here that while matters of faith did in fact separate religious Independents from many religious Presbyterians, the differences between the two were not nearly as great as has often been suggested. Indeed, one is frequently struck by their similarities. The Independents who go off to the new world to establish a pure church find themselves in sympathy with the position taken by the Presbyterians who remain behind. We have the spectacle of the Scottish minister Samuel Rutherford praising the work of the New England Congregational minister John Cotton. "When I read through the treatise of the *Keys of the Kingdom,"* stated Rutherford, "I thought it an easy labor for an universal pacification, he comes so near unto us." [53] The late Professor Perry Miller has pointed out in his *Orthodoxy in Massachusetts* how

> the party in England which had begun as the advocate of Congregationalism was swept by the rush of events into upholding a policy which had been pronounced by the New England system to be eternally heretical in religion and utterly intolerable in society.[54]

The policy that Scots Presbyterian and New England Puritan joined hands across the sea to oppose can be summed up in one word: toleration. Yet paradoxically, "the rush of events" in England had a softening effect—to the extent that some Scotsmen demonstrated a willingness to tone down their former rigidity. In answer to charges made by the Independents and various sectaries that the Presbyterians would persecute anyone who deviated from strict Presbyterianism, David Buchanan wrote:

> They cry out against the rigidness of Presbyterial government, as aforesaid, to make the people believe that it will tie them to such a strictness and rigidity, or austerity, that all Christian liberty will be taken away from them. Wherein they do lie most abominably against the practice of all the Reformed churches where the government hath place, namely in Scotland and France, where if there be anything amiss of this kind, it is toward leniency rather than austerity.[55]

Buchanan's own position may not have been truly representative of every Scottish Presbyterian, but the foregoing quotation reveals that not all Scots ignored the needs of their English brethren. In January 1645 George Gillespie, speaking before the Westminster Assembly, said regarding the religious Independents: "I wish they prove to be as unwilling to divide from us as we have been unwilling to divide from them." Then he added, "I wish that instead of toleration there may be a mutual endeavor for a happy accommodation." [56] Obviously many Scots realized that a Presbyterian arrangement in England could never be as restrictive as the one in their own country; a certain amount of flexibility would have to be permitted to accommodate responsible Puritan groups.[57] Thus, while a crucial issue dividing Presbyterian from Independent remained that of toleration, it was never a question of complete toleration versus none at all. The more realistic Scottish divines, men like Gillespie for example, appreciated the need for compromise with the Independents. This would, of necessity, mean a modification of the English discipline. Furthermore, the attitude of the Independents regarding toleration contained ambiguities. The question to which we now have to direct ourselves is: Were the Independents committed to complete toleration?

In September 1644 it appeared as if the leaders of the war party (the future "Independent" party) did in fact advocate full toleration. "The great shot of Cromwell and Vane," wrote Baillie at that time, "is to have a liberty for all religions without any exceptions." [58] And a year later, in November 1645, Baillie again reported that the "Independents" "expressed their desire for toleration, not only for themselves but to other sects." [59] Yet in their introduction to John Cotton's *The Keys of the Kingdom of Heaven,* printed in June 1644, Thomas Goodwin and Philip Nye placed an important restriction on religious freedom. These two Independent divines supported their American colleague in his belief that a synod should be furnished

> not only with ability to give counsel and advice, but further . . . with a ministerial power and authority to determine, declare and enjoin such things as may tend to the reducing such congregations to right order and peace.[60]

Goodwin and Nye did not specify exactly what they might consider proper grounds for action by the synod. Apparently clarification would be postponed for a more propitious occasion. Nevertheless, the fact remains that at a time when religious Independents became associated in the minds of contemporaries with the doctrine of toleration, they themselves had already begun to qualify that principle.

The most crucial period for religious reform during the Civil War was the year 1645-1646. Most of the significant religious legislation passed through Parliament at this time. Yet for a large portion of the year the religious Independents actually provided no opposition to the Presbyterians, and they did virtually nothing to prevent the Westminster Assembly from hammering out one plank after another of a Presbyterian church government.

At the end of March 1645 the Assembly of Divines had formally requested the dissenting brethren to form a committee in order "to bring in the whole frame of their judgments concerning government in a body with their grounds and reasons."[61] The Independents acceded to this request, and thereupon removed themselves from the assembly to draw up a complete statement of their principles. They were gone for almost eight months. Their absence provided their opponents, the Presbyterians, with a marvelous opportunity. With the exception of the few individualistic Erastians, no other organized religious faction had the strength to delay the passage of Presbyterian measures. "Church work here," wrote Baillie in May 1645,

> goes on with less difficulty than it was wont. The Assembly having put the Independents to show what positively is their judgment in things controverted, we have been quit of their number these six or seven weeks.[62]

The Presbyterians, of course, used their unchallenged supremacy to rush their measures through the assembly. In June 1645 the remaining divines made an assertion of *jure divino* in regard to excommunication. "We claim our power of Jesus Christ," they informed Parliament.[63] During the following month Robert Baillie happily reported that the divines had "sent up to both Houses the whole body of the church government, so it is once out of the Assembly's hands."[64] And this same letter to Scotland carried the welcome information that London was rapidly becoming a Presbyterian city. "Blessed be God," Baillie declared, "all the ministers of London are for us."[65]

Why the dissenting brethren decided to absent themselves from the Assembly of Divines, thereby giving the Presbyterians a free hand, remains a bit of a mystery. The Independents themselves never provided an explanation for their behavior. Perhaps they realized that their former delaying tactics could no longer hold off the inevitable. They may have thought that a strong statement of purpose of their own would convert Parliament to their side. But in all likelihood, the Independents were simply outmaneuvered by the Presbyterians.

Whatever the reason, it cannot be denied that the Independents had made a serious blunder. They encountered a great deal of difficulty in framing their statement, and it became evident that no agreement could be reached because of disputes among themselves.[66] Quite likely, different conceptions concerning the degree of toleration to be advocated presented a stumbling block. We know, for example, that Philip Nye was less favorably disposed toward congregational autonomy than John Goodwin, as their divergent views came to light during the Whitehall debates of 1648-1649.[67]

Simply in terms of tactics, the Independents had created for themselves a dilemma which proved very difficult to resolve. If they came out strongly for complete religious freedom they might very well lose the good will of moderate opinion in Parliament, just those members whom they would presumably want to win over by their statement of aims. If, on the other hand, they restricted toleration in 1645 (as they were to do in 1649), the Independents would have to sever their ties with the sectaries, many of whom held influential positions in the army. A stand in favor of limited toleration might even alienate Cromwell. Robert Baillie recognized the problem facing the dissenting brethren. He wrote:

> We hope shortly to get the Independents put to it to declare themselves either to be for the rest of the sectaries, or against them. If they declare against them, they will be but a small, inconsiderable company; if for them, all honest men will cry out upon them for separating from all the Reformed churches to join with Anabaptists and Libertines.[68]

In the end the Independents proved unable to reach a decision, and not knowing how to extricate themselves from a predicament of their own making, they retreated. Instead of publishing their views as had been planned, on October 13, 1645 they issued a declaration explaining why they could not bring forth their statement at this time: they would not produce it, in effect, because they did not wish to do so.[69] In this rather blunt fashion the Independents attempted to brazen their way out of their dilemma, rather than face the consequences of a premature declaration of purpose. They had made the best of a complex situation, but nonetheless had lost ground. Their continuing absence from the Westminster Assembly had permitted the Presbyterians to rush through measures which would make it more difficult than ever for an Independent church government to be established in England.

Approximately three years after their nonstatement, the Independents did have an opportunity to present their position in detail. At the Whitehall debates, which took place at the moment when the army had purged Parliament and had begun to make ready to try the king, the various Independents explained their ideas on toleration. Henry Ireton, Cromwell's son-in-law and the spokesman for the army Independents, told the assembled persons, including some Levellers, that he would never accept the separation of church and state. He said further that freedom to practice one's religion ought to be limited by the civil authority. In forming a political order, Ireton argued, a certain measure of power is granted to the magistrate (or legislature): "we may upon the same ground, without further prejudice to the inward man, refer to them [the magistrates] a power of determining as to the outward man what they will allow or suffer in matters of religion." [70] Ireton implied that there existed a whole category of religious practices which came under the heading of "false worship," and which magistrates should forbid. Philip Nye, present at the debate, seconded Ireton and added:

> Then [if the end of a commonwealth be to provide] for common good, and if things of God, [and blessings] appertaining to them, be a good to be wished; if they do not [only] tend to that [common good], but prevent evil and [the attendant] judgments of God, I know nothing but in conclusion there may be some power made up in the magistrate as may attend to it.[71]

The "middle way" of the Independents in both religion and politics did not go far enough for the Levellers, who decided to boycott the debates at

Whitehall.[72] Too moderate for religious extremists, but too extreme for rigid Presbyterians, the Independents remained a separate force in English religious and political affairs. With the passage of three centuries the differences between Presbyterian and Independent may seem to have been minor, and it is sometimes difficult to comprehend why an accommodation could not have been arranged. As we have observed earlier, the two groups in time proved to be divided less by questions of substance than by those of degree. While High Presbyterians devoted most of their energy and time to combating the Independents, it would appear with hindsight that they, and the Scots in particular, exhausted themselves fighting the wrong enemy.

It has already been noted that not very many religious Independents could be found in Parliament, yet few of the Scots seemed to realize this. Despite an occasional reference to the Erastians in Parliament, one receives the impression from Baillie's letters that he considered the Independents the greatest threat to the establishment of Presbyterians, Scottish style. He certainly mentioned them more frequently than he did the Erastians, and the same can be said of the letters from the Scottish commissioners.[73]

To a greater extent than did the lay commissioners from the Estates, the Scottish divines saw the Civil War in religious terms. During the first years their horizons had been limited to the world of the Westminster Assembly; and in the assembly, with the exception of the annoyingly condescending speeches delivered by John Selden, their main opposition came from the Independents. Consequently the divines directed their fire at the dissenting brethren, who interfered with their efforts to establish the true church. In reality the Independents could do little more than cause delay in the assembly, and the Scots knew this. History and truth, so they believed, were on the side of the Presbyterians. Eventually the Independents would have to stop talking, at which point the assembly would give its approval to a Scottish form of Presbyterianism, and the subject would be settled for all time. Perennial optimists, convinced that the Lord would surely crown their efforts, the Scots scarcely gave thought to what lay beyond the ratification which would be given to a Presbyterian church by the Westminster Assembly.

An early indication the Scots had that there was more to establishing Presbyterianism in England than securing the approval of the ministers came in August 1644. During this month the Commons returned the ordinance for ordination to the assembly with the stipulation that the measure should be only provisional, and not fixed forever.[74] Although visibly disappointed by the Commons' refusal to honor this ordinance with the sanctification of *jure divino,* the Scots did not regard the alteration as a major setback. The legislation passed in October, but three months later, in January 1645, the two houses took steps to appease the Scots. They abolished the Book of Common Prayer and established a Directory of Public Worship in its place.[75] Later in the month the Commons passed two more resolutions favorable to Scottish Presbyterianism. "Many particular congregations may be under one Presbyterial government," they resolved on the 14th; and a week later the lower house declared that the new church would be "governed by congregational, classical and synodical assemblies," and that the latter should consist of both provincial and national assemblies.[76]

The Scottish commissioners became greatly encouraged. On January 23 they wrote to the General Assembly of the kirk that the measures aforementioned "are three or four witnesses to prove that the Lord hath done great things for us, whereof we are glad and which make us like them that dream." [77] So overjoyed were they that they recommended immediate ratification of the new Directory of Worship by the General Assembly.

The kirk responded without delay. They decided to accept the commissioners' recommendation even though they had reservations:

> We still conceive and believe the order and practice of our own Kirk to be most agreeable and suitable to the word of God, the example of our Lord Jesus Christ and the nature of that Heavenly feast and table.[78]

In other words, the recent Parliamentary ordinances might be considered acceptable, but the Scots wanted to make it clear that these ordinances did not match the Scottish conception of perfection, i.e., their own church. For the sake of harmony with their English allies, the divines in Edinburgh went ahead and gave their approval.[79]

This magnanimous gesture on the part of the Scots may very well have proven their own undoing. For having once demonstrated their willingness to compromise, even slightly, in order to reach an agreement, the impression must have gone out that they would compromise even further when necessary. This impression received reinforcement when George Gillespie returned to London from Scotland in the spring of 1645. He told his English brethren that "the Directory [was] accepted with great joy and contentment, both to the General Assembly and Parliament, [and was] approved in both without one contrary vote in either."[80]

After having given the Scots the idea that their heart was in the right place, Parliament began to ignore the need for further reform. During the spring of 1645 the House of Commons delayed the passage of legislation affecting the church, much to the annoyance of the Scots. On the 10th of March 1645 a group of Presbyterian ministers from London petitioned the two houses to grant power to the clergy to deny the sacraments to ignorant and scandalous persons.[81] Taking the content of the petition into consideration the Commons, a fortnight later, resolved that there were some persons so grossly ignorant and notoriously scandalous "that they shall not be admitted to the sacrament of the Lord's Supper." This same resolution the Commons repeated twice more, the last time on April 1.[82]

Having done this, Parliament then decided to rest. On April 1 the Commons presented the Westminster Assembly with an assignment designed to keep the divines busy for some time. They requested that the Assembly provide an extensive definition of the categories of persons who should not be allowed to take the Lord's Supper. And if this was not enough to tie up the assembly for the next months, the Commons also resolved:

> That it be referred to the Assembly of Divines to set down, in particular, what they conceive to be such a competent measure of understanding concerning the state of man by creation and by his fall; the redemption of Jesus Christ; the way and means to apply Christ and His benefits; the nature and necessity of faith, repentence and a godly life; the nature and use of sacraments; and the condition of man after this life, without which, none shall be admitted to the sacrament of the Lord's Supper.[83]

As the Commons undoubtedly realized, the answers to their questions would not be produced overnight. Experience had already shown that the members of the Westminster Assembly had difficulty reaching agreement among themselves on relatively minor matters. To provide precise responses to the weighty queries posed by Parliament might well prove impossible. At best the process would slow down the Assembly considerably. This effect, evidently desired, was achieved. "Our progress in the Assembly is but small," wrote Baillie at this time. "We fell in a labyrinth of a catalogue of sins for which people must be kept from the sacrament and ministers be deposed."[84]

While the divines wrestled with the intricacies of theological definitions, Parliament, after a month's respite from religious matters, again raised the issue of suspension from the Lord's Supper. On May 3 the Grand Committee on Religion reported that the eldership of every congregation had the authority to suspend scandalous persons from the sacrament. Within a week the Lords confirmed this idea in principle.[85] But their confirmation resolved nothing, and the matter was brought up for discussion in the Grand Committee on numerous occasions. Within the committee the Erastians posed a serious threat to the passage of the measure. John Selden, the most articulate and knowledgeable of the Erastians in Parliament, called for revisions on the ground that, if ratified in its present form, the ordinance would give ministers too much power.[86]

Three months passed without any action being taken, and understandably the Presbyterian divines grew rather impatient with this lack of progress. On August 8 the assembly delivered a petition to Parliament "concerning the keeping of notorious, ignorant and scandalous persons from the sacrament of the Lord's Supper." The divines reminded Parliament "that there is not a matter of higher concernment for the glory of God and peace of this church."[87] However, Parliament did not respond, so three weeks later more pressure was applied. This time the ministers of London and Westminster delivered a petition imploring Parliament to pass the necessary legislation. Another two months had to go by before Parliament decided that the time had become ripe. On October 20, 1645 the ordinance concerning suspension from the Lord's Supper in cases of ignorance and scandal finally became law.[88]

This ordinance, for which the Scots and their Presbyterian allies had worked so strenuously, turned out to be far removed from the Presbyterian measure that they had envisaged. Any person suspended from the Lord's Supper by the elders of his congregation might petition the church hierarchy, which of course was the procedure in Scotland; there, once an appeal was rejected by the Scottish General Assembly, an individual had no further recourse. But according to Parliament's ordinance, if one did not obtain satisfaction from the church leaders, he could then appeal over their heads to Parliament. Thus, in the very crucial matter of degrees of authority along the hierarchical scale, Parliament retained the highest rank: in all disputes it would be the supreme court of appeals in the land.

As had been the case with previous enactments, Parliament made no mention of the eternal authority *(jure divino),* which justified suspending persons from the sacrament. The deletion of these words, whose insertion had been requested by the assembly, was not merely an oversight. Whitelock tells us that a majority of members "opposed it [*jure divino*] as giving them [the ministers] too much power of persecution." [89] Henceforth Parliament could either add or subtract reasons for suspension from the Lord's Supper as it saw fit—without having to consult anyone. In the final version of the ordinance this power, which Parliament reserved for itself, found expression in the "negative clause that there should be no other cause of suspension but those such as should be allowed by both Houses of Parliament." [90] In other words, the Presbyterian clergy would not be given a free hand to harass the dissenting brethren or even the sectaries. This "negative clause" formed the crux of the Parliamentary Erastian position, since it inhibited the free action of the ecclesiastical court by making the determination of sin a matter for Parliamentary supervision.

The October ordinance proved not to be the end of the subject of suspensions from the Lord's Supper. Just a week after its passage the Commons issued a new order to the assembly, calling on the divines to provide the House with a list of "such other notorious and scandalous sins in particular for which they desired that persons guilty thereof may be suspended from the sacrament of the Lord's Supper." [91] The key phrase here is "in particular." Its inclusion meant that Parliament refused once more to grant the presbyteries a general jurisdiction over categorizing of sins. This power would remain with the two houses. Furthermore, the new request made it appear as if the whole business was beginning once again, delays and all. Thus on November 12 the Westminster Assembly presented the Commons with its "humble advice and request touching some new particulars to be added to the catalogue of scandalous offenders"; and accordingly the Commons referred the matter to the Grand Committee for Religion, just as had been done before.[92]

Four months later, on March 14, 1646, the second ordinance for exclusion from the sacrament became law.[93] Its character was even more Erastian than that of the first ordinance, as it provided for Parliamentary commissioners to reside in every county of England. These commissioners would actually have the power to supervise the execution of the law by the eldership of each county, to make sure that the elders followed Parliament's dictates. Not only would this provision serve to undercut the autonomy of the local elders, it would seriously weaken the authority of the ecclesiastical hierarchy as well.

England had not heard the last of the question of suspension from the sacrament. A final ordinance passed both houses on June 5, 1646, which did not add or detract significantly from the previous ones. But the fact that Parliament felt it necessary to issue this last measure indicated that the subject of exclusion from the Lord's Supper had not really been settled until then.[94]

The finished product of Parliament's long deliberations was, as we have noted before, an Erastian form of Presbyterianism. Naturally enough, the Scots and the other Presbyterian divines felt cheated by the final settlement. But what remains surprising is the manner in which the Scots interpreted their defeat. "This is a trick of the Independents' intervention," wrote an angered Baillie in March 1646, "to enervate and disgrace all our government, in which they have been assisted by the lawyers and the Erastian party."[95] To the very end, the Scots placed the blame for their demise on a plot; and of course the Independents took first place as the villains of the piece. "The sectarian party is very malicious and powerful," Baillie stated in the same letter. "They have carried the House of Commons and are like also to carry the House of Lords to spoil much our church government."[96]

It is clear that, even after all they had been through, the Scots did not appreciate the nature of the opposition to Presbyterianism in England. They chose to blame the Independents for the creation of an Erastian church, never explaining why the latter should favor Erastianism over Independency. Nor could they possibly demonstrate how a handful of religious Independents might inflict their will on a Parliament which most certainly was non-Independent in religion. The "assist" given to the Independents by the Erastian lawyers, as Baillie would have it, understated the role of the latter and exaggerated that of the former. For the true story was that an Independent minority followed the lead of an Erastian majority, thereby keeping in step with the mainstream of Parliamentary politics–a feat which the Covenanters failed to match.

NOTES

1. C.J., IV, p. 37.
2. Wodrow MSS, LXVII, fol. 31.
3. Meikle, p. 61.
4. C.S.P.D., 1645, p. 392.
5. C.J., IV, p. 52; L.J., VII, p. 217.
6. L.J., VII, pp. 619-620.
7. C.S.P.D., 1645, pp. 315-316.
8. Dewes, 166, fol. 180.
9. Meikle, p. 69. For a full account of Scottish receipts, see David Stevenson, "The Financing of the Cause of the Covenanters," *Scottish Historical Review,* LI (1972), pp. 89-123.
10. C.J., IV, pp. 96-110.
11. Sabran, PRO, 31/3/76, fol. 176.
12. Baillie, II, pp. 269-270.
13. Dr. Valerie Pearl suggests that the Scots formed an alliance with the peace group in the fall of 1644 (op. cit., p. 516). But this ignores the disagreement between the two regarding ending negotiations at

Uxbridge; it does not explain either Scottish neutrality while Essex was being removed, or their failure to oppose the creation of a New Model Army at the start.

14. *Mercurius Aulicus,* February 27, 1645.
15. Ibid.
16. Ibid.
17. Buchanan, p. 59.
18. Holles, pp. 20-21.
19. *Vindiciae Veritatis* speaks about the Covenanters joining an alliance with Essex and his party: "The envy that both had against the new-modelled army bring them to agree *Ineodem tertio* at first, and afterwards to grow better acquainted, and go on together in other designs, and correspond in them also . . ." (part II, p. 97).
20. Dewes, 166, fol. 181v.
21. Ibid.
22. Ibid.
23. See above, chap. IV.
24. Sabran, PRO, 31/3/76, fol. 120v.
25. Buchanan, pp. 66-67.
26. Most of the leaders of the peace group were Erastians. Some, like Denzil Holles and the Earl of Essex, were favorably disposed toward episcopacy (Clarendon, I, p. 309). Sir Philip Stapleton's eulogizer tells us that regarding religion, he was not "easily engaged into anything of change." T.T.E. 409 (3). John Maynard not only had reservations against taking the Covenant in September 1643; two years later he served as a teller in support of an Erastian church government (C.J. III, p. 259, IV, p. 303; Dewes, 166, fol. 7).
27. Evidence for this is the fact the Scots never reproached the peace party for their support of the Erastian settlement of 1646. This is in sharp contrast to their vehement denunciations of the war party's espousal of accommodation of tender consciences in September 1644, and the subsequent rupture of their alliance with the war party.
28. Baillie, for example, regarded Cromwell's attack on Manchester in November 1644 as "a high and mighty plot of the Independent party to have gotten an army for themselves under Cromwell" (II, p. 246;

see also ibid., pp. 279-281, 287). *Vindiciae Veritatis* also commented about the Scots' tendency to call M.P.s who opposed Scottish Presbyterianism "Independents" (part I, p. 9).

29. Even contemporaries found these designations confusing. See, for example, John Harris, *The Royal Quarrel,* 1648, T.T., E. 426 (11).
30. See most notably J. H. Hexter, "The Problem of the Presbyterian Independents," in *Reappraisals in History* (Aberdeen, 1962), pp. 163-184; also David Underdown, "The Independents Reconsidered," in *Journal of British Studies,* vol. III, pp. 57-84; and Valerie Pearl, "The Royal Independents' in the English Civil War," *Transactions of the Royal Historical Society,* 5th Series, vol. 18 (1968), pp. 69-96.
31. Hexter, op. cit., p. 172.
32. Baillie, II, pp. 265-266. Another implication which can be drawn from Baillie's statement is that, as a Scottish minister, he still retained hopes—however baseless in fact—of a pure Presbyterian church settlement.
33. Ibid., pp. 360-361. Baillie became so enraged at Coleman that he described him as "a man reasonably learned, but stupid and inconsiderate, half a peasant, and of small estimation."
34. T.T., E. 294 (14).
35. Yonge, 18, 780, fol. 86.
36. T.T., E. 298 (12).
37. H. R. Trevor-Roper, "The Fast Sermons of the Long Parliament," in *Essays in British History* (London, 1964), p. 116. One last invitation was extended on September 5, 1645 for an extraordinary fast related to the difficulties of the Scottish nation. See John F. Wilson, *Pulpit in Parliament* (Princeton, 1969), p. 85.
38. *Acts and Ordinances,* I, pp. 852-855.
39. Notably by S. R. Gardiner and by W. A. Shaw, *A History of the English Church during the Civil War and under the Commonwealth,* 2 vols. (London, 1900).
40. Baillie, II, p. 362.
41. L.J., VIII, p. 202.
42. C.J., IV, pp. 95, 257. Strode died in September 1645.

43. Baillie, II, p. 359; C.J., IV, p. 228; D.N.B.
44. Baillie, II, p. 237; C.J., IV, p. 213; D.N.B.
45. Shaw, II, p. 404; D.N.B.
46. Clarendon, III, p. 497.
47. T.T., E. 409 (3).
48. Baillie, II, p. 362. The city on March 14, 1646, delivered their third petition to Parliament, but when told by the House of Commons not to present any more petitions of that kind, they meekly obeyed; Whitacre, fol. 520.
49. The relevant pieces of legislation were the following: ordinance regulating the election of elders, August 19, 1645, *Acts and Ordinances,* I pp. 749-754; ordinance concerning suspension from the sacrament, October 20, 1645, ibid., pp. 789-797; ordinance for keeping of scandalous persons from the sacrament (and) the enabling of congregations for the choice of elders, etc., March 14, 1646, ibid., pp. 833-838; ordinance to exclude improper persons from the sacrament, June 5, 1646, ibid., pp. 852-855.
50. T.T., 669 f. 10 (68).
51. C.S.P.D., 1645, pp. 179-180.
52. C.J., IV, p. 493; S. W. Carruthers, *Everyday Work of the Westminster Assembly* (Philadelphia, 1943), p. 57; A. F. Mitchell and J. Struthers, *Minutes of the Westminster Assembly of Divines* (Edinburgh, 1874), p. 214.
53. Mitchell and Struthers, op. cit., p. 60.
54. Perry Miller, *Orthodoxy in Massachusetts* (Boston, 1959), p. 273.
55. Buchanan, pp. 86-87.
56. Mitchell and Struthers, op. cit., p. 28.
57. David Stevenson, "The Radical Party in the Kirk, 1637-45," *Journal of Ecclesiastical History,* vol. XXV (1974), pp. 135-165.
58. Baillie, II, p. 230. Baillie believed that political and religious "Independents" were identical.
59. Ibid., p. 326.
60. Deletion in the original. A. S. P. Woodhouse (ed.), *Puritanism and Liberty* (Chicago, 1951), p. 296.

61. Mitchell and Struthers, op. cit., p. 132.
62. Baillie, II, p. 270.
63. Mitchell and Struthers, op. cit., p. 72.
64. Baillie, II, p. 299.
65. Ibid.
66. Ibid., pp. 317-318.
67. Woodhouse, pp. 125-178.
68. Baillie, II, pp. 229-230.
69. T.T., E. 309 (4).
70. Woodhouse, p. 133.
71. Ibid., p. 160.
72. T. C. Pease, *The Leveller Movement* (Baltimore, 1916), pp. 263-264.
73. Baillie, II, pp. 336-337. The Erastian threat was not appreciated by the Scots until Coleman's speech in July 1645. See also Meikle, passim.
74. C.J., III, p. 592.
75. *Acts and Ordinances,* I, pp. 582-607.
76. C.J., IV, pp. 22, 28.
77. T.T., E. 294 (4).
78. Ibid.
79. Ibid.
80. Mitchell and Struthers, op. cit., p. 77.
81. Whitelock, I, p. 403.
82. C.J., IV, pp. 89, 92, 95.
83. Ibid., p. 95.
84. Baillie, II, p. 286.
85. L.J., VII, p. 362.
86. Dewes, 166, fol. 183.
87. C.J., IV, p. 234.
88. *Acts and Ordinances,* I, pp. 789-797.
89. Whitelock, I, p. 493.
90. Whitacre, fol. 471.
91. C.J., IV, p. 324.
92. Ibid., p. 339.
93. *Acts and Ordinances,* I, pp. 833-838.

94. Ibid., pp. 852-855.
95. Baillie, II, p. 357. The Scots' resistance to the Erastian government, i.e., their attempt to rally the city in opposition to the settlement, also failed.
96. Ibid.

Epilogue

The Erastian form of Presbyterianism established by the English Parliament represented a major setback for those Scots who had wished to gain security for their homeland by creating parallel ecclesiastical institutions in England. A serious limitation that the Covenanters found in the new church government was its seeming inability to restrain the spread of schism and heresy that continued unabated during 1645 and 1646. The surprising performance of Parliament's army in the field provided greater respectability for Cromwell's doctrine of toleration, while the New Model itself came to symbolize the very personification of religious diversity. The growing prestige of this army began to give concern to the Covenanters because of its subversive example, as well as through its potential for independent action.

The New Model Army's great victories, first at Naseby and then in the West Country, totally eliminated the need for Scottish assistance. In reality the Covenanters had contributed virtually nothing to the military campaign after their belated capture of Newcastle in October 1644. Quite clearly, by the summer of 1645 they had become superfluous. In fact, during this time the Scottish army in England stationed itself in the north, far from any Royalist troops, and began to live off the already exhausted resources of the region. In the process an enmity was created toward the Scots which became quite pronounced,[1] and was to continue for years afterward.

Ironically, the removal of a Royalist military threat in England coincided with the rise of Montrose in Scotland. His spectacular success in the summer of 1645 humiliated the Covenanters, especially when he gained control of the entire country after the Battle of Kilsyth. Thus the quest for security which enticed the Covenanters to intervene in an English Civil War appeared totally lost, because of countermeasures taken by Charles I to deal with this same involvement. Moreover, the humiliating experience with Montrose further reduced English respect for the Scots.

When General Leven defeated Montrose at Philiphaugh in September 1645, and the threat posed by him was removed, the Scots began addressing themselves to the crucial matter of arranging peace with the king. Unfortunately, when the Covenanters began calling for a treaty they encountered a new reality in England. Their status in that country had declined precipitously and Parliament refused to heed any of their requests. During the fall of 1645 a growing number of English M.P.s openly advocated the disbandonment of the Scottish army, while veiled threats concerning New Model Army maneuvers in the north of England some months later added to the pressure for an immediate withdrawal of their forces.[2]

The construction of fresh peace terms in the spring of 1646 gave further indication that the Covenanters were being ignored by the English Parliament. Nothing dramatizes the Scots' declining position in England more than the fact that in 1644 they had drawn up the Uxbridge Treaty largely by themselves, while in 1646 their commissioners had great difficulty altering a phrase in the Newcastle Propositions.[3] The new treaty not only placed more stringent restrictions on the Crown, specifically reducing royal power; it also eliminated the important and permanent role the Covenanters had hoped to continue playing in English affairs.[4] All mention of joint committees to enforce the settlement and to preserve the future peace were carefully omitted from the propositions. In dropping the concept of conjoint institutions, the new treaty further weakened the Scottish attempt to attain security.

By the spring of 1646 it appeared that the Covenanters had lost all leverage in English affairs and, as a result, the possibility of salvaging concrete gains from their intervention in England now seemed rather dim. Out of the mood of pessimism which pervaded Scottish thinking at this juncture emerged a fantastic new scheme, which would have had the king seek the protection of the Scottish army. This was a desperate maneuver, but it held out the hope of transforming the present situation by providing the Covenanters once again with a strong bargaining position.

When the scheme was finally carried out in May 1646 it proved to be a serious mistake not only for the king, who became a virtual prisoner, but for the Scots as well, for they gained little from their prize possession. That the king's flight to the Scottish army had such a small impact upon the outcome of events resulted from inadequate planning by the participants, and by the failure to anticipate consequences realistically. The Scots had hoped to convert Charles to Presbyterianism, thereby achieving their main goals, security and salvation. The king had no such intentions, for in actuality he hated the Scottish religion, equating it with permanent rebellion.[5] As a result of this fundamental conflict of aims, the king's flight to the Scots was doomed to fail even before it took place.

The anti-Scottish sentiment which had been rising throughout 1645 reached its highest point when the news became known that the Scots army now controlled the royal person. The Independent party made a telling point when they argued that to demobilize Parliament's army at this time would be a "betrayal of the Kingdom." [6] Consequently, in the fall of 1646, despite the fact that the Royalist army had all but disappeared, an ordinance passed Parliament extending the New Model for six more months. With the Scottish forces still in England, the lower house did not even bother to divide on the motion.[7]

Paradoxically, it was the Covenanters' allies, the political Presbyterians, who now stood to profit the most from their Scottish brethren leaving the country. The strong anti-Scottish feeling had rubbed off on the Presbyterians and, in part accounts for their relatively poor standing during most of 1646. They began to recognize that the continued presence of the

Scots in England had become a liability. Consequently, it was the moderates who convinced the Covenanters both to leave and to surrender the king to Parliament.[8] Holles and Stapleton also helped Parliament to arrive at the amount (£400,000) to be paid as compensation, and then they encouraged the Scottish commissioners to be satisfied with this amount, for they conceived it "altogether impossible to obtain a greater sum." [9]

Toward the end of October the Scottish leadership concluded that Charles would have to be returned to the English. The pressure to do so had become very great. Their allies, the political Presbyterians, urged them more forcefully than anyone else to surrender him. In Scotland the kirk had stepped up its campaign, begun that September, to turn over the king whom, they now recognized, would never accept their church. By November the commissioners of the kirk sent a remonstrance to the Scottish Parliament, which ministers read in all pulpits, "showing the danger of bringing the King to Scotland unless he secured religion and the peace of both Kingdoms," [10] a rather unlikely prospect.

A last-ditch attempt in Scotland was made by the moderate Royalists, led by the Marquis of Hamilton and his brother, the Earl of Lanark, in December 1646 to resist giving up the king until firm assurances for his safety were obtained. But the heads of the kirk realized that unless Charles subscribed to the Covenant and promised to establish a Presbyterian church throughout his kingdoms, Scotland would gain nothing by defying Parliament. They produced a declaration predicting "the hazard of a bloody war" with England if the Scots failed to relinquish their prisoners.[11] With the Marquis of Argyll firmly in control, the Scottish Estates on December 17, 1646 passed a resolution refusing to allow the king to be brought to Scotland, and making it unlawful to espouse his cause.[12] As long as Charles remained opposed to the Covenant, and as long as the kirk preserved its moral and political leadership, Scotland would be governed without Charles I and he would be left to his own devices in England.

The only issue remaining to be negotiated between the two countries was the manner in which the English Parliament chose to pay the Covenanting army. Throughout December the appointed Parliamentary committee worked out specific details with the Scottish commissioners. The Scots at this point strove to avoid serious disagreements, and therefore conceded almost every contentious item. A newsletter from London attributed their newly found tactfulness and circumspection to their fear that Parliament might withhold some of the promised money.[13] But they need not have been concerned. An ordinance passed both houses on December 10, providing for the initial sum of £200,000 to be realized upon the sale of bishops' lands.[14] If anything, most M.P.s were as desirous of concluding arrangements as were their Scottish counterparts.

Taking the lead, now as before, in encouraging the commissioners to resolve all matters promptly, was the Presbyterian party. They had begun anticipating the advantages which they would accrue when the unpopular Scots left. As predicted, the imminent Scottish departure served to increase their own political importance. In December and January several observers commented on how the Presbyterians had gained in stature during the past weeks.[15] A dialectical connection now existed: the sooner the Covenanters departed, the faster the Presbyterians would take charge of the English political scene. So anxious had the moderates become for an immediate withdrawal of Covenanting troops that some of the commissioners began wondering whether their friends could still be trusted.[16] However, the Presbyterian leadership proved correct. Once the Scottish army left England, their party did in fact emerge as the dominant force in the Long Parliament. Whether they also controlled Parliament's own army turned out to be a different question.

With final provisions concluded by late December, Edinburgh had to assume the responsibility for surrendering the king. One last appeal by the Estates was sent to Charles on the 24th, requesting that he assent to all the Newcastle Propositions and swear to the Covenant. But it lacked conviction.[17] The king's fate had already been sealed. Less than a week later, the Scottish commissioners in London took their leave of England. They received a rather qualified statement of appreciation from the English Parliament,[18] thus ending a significant episode in Anglo-Scottish relations. On January 14, 1647 the Estates officially notified the king that his continued intransigence left them with no choice but to turn him over to his English subjects. The kingdom of Scotland, they also informed him, would continue to be governed "without your Majesty, as hath been done these years by-past."[19]

Finally, on January 16 the Scottish Parliament declared its intention to go ahead with their pledge to the English "in regard of his Majesty's not giving a satisfactory answer to the propositions as asked, and out of their earnest desire to keep a right understanding betwixt these Kingdoms to prevent new troubles. . . ." An appendage to this declaration expressed the Scots' hope that all efforts would be made to further press the king to accede to the propositions, and "that there be no harm, prejudice, injury, nor violence done to his Royal person"; and furthermore, that there be no change in government nor should there be any interference with the lawful succession to the Crown.[20]

The Argyll forces encountered no difficulty in carrying through these last measures. Hamilton and Lanark raised their voices in "horror," we are told, but they failed to do anything else to stop the Covenanters. When the declaration of January 16 received the approval of the Estates, most moderate Royalists did not even bother to cast negative votes. In fact, a number of them gave in to the pressure and sided with the majority.[21] Quite obviously, Hamilton had neglected to organize his supporters to fight this rather crucial step, demonstrating once again an unwillingness to contemplate a strong stand against those who dominated political and religious affairs in Scotland. Certainly he never considered extraordinary operations, such as military resistance of the Montrose variety, to oppose an action which many individuals regarded as illegal and immoral. This behavior led some Royalists to conclude that the duke and his brother were in league with the Argyll party at this time.[22] In reality, the Hamiltons were following the pattern they had established for themselves earlier in the decade. They would use parliamentary means to neutralize the Covenanters, but would never employ extralegal measures to accomplish their purposes. Therefore, to the very end a "political consensus" worked against the king's interests in Scotland.

On January 30, 1647, exactly a fortnight after the declaration of the Estates, the Scottish commissioners at Newcastle delivered over Charles I to the army of the English Parliament without incident. The sum of £100,000 was paid to the Scots on that date, and four days later, in a second installment, an equal amount was given to the appointed agents from Edinburgh. In a week's time the last Scottish soldier crossed over the border and all fortresses held by their army were relinquished.[23] The intervention of the Covenanters in the first Civil War had come to a close.

In Royalist circles in England this willingness to yield their sovereign for money rendered Scotland's name "odious." [24] Yet reality was more complex than this simple judgment. The king had resisted every reasonable effort to compromise, despite repeated Scottish warnings that unless he make concessions they could not bring him to their country, and risk unrest at home as well as a disastrous conflict with the stronger English forces. What could be gained by the inevitable bloodshed? Almost inexplicably Charles refused to examine the requirements of his possible benefactors, insisting only on his own hatred for their religion. As a result, he did nothing concrete to hinder the transactions which decided his fate. Perhaps he hoped that something miraculous would turn up to assist his cause. In January 1647 no such prospect appeared to be forthcoming.

The decision to abandon their king failed to create any immediate problem for the Covenanters at home. Ill consequences which some Royalists predicted did not come to pass, for in many ways the move was a popular one. The opportunity for lasting peace seemed much more important to a majority of Scots than further entanglement in the labyrinth of English affairs, which carried the risk of permanent war. Even the kirk, previously the leading advocate of righteous intervention, had reversed itself and now led those calling for retrenchment. Possessing little sympathy for a recalcitrant monarch, the church hierarchy in Scotland had become reconciled to an inferior ecclesiastical government south of the border, recognizing pragmatically that this was probably the best settlement under existing circumstances.[25] In Scotland at this time the wish to be involved in England was limited to a handful. More than a year would pass before the Duke of Hamilton could mobilize support for another try. Although the motives and many of the personnel would be different then, the results were to be worse.

By and large, Scottish intervention in England during the first Civil War has to be viewed as a major setback. Almost every aim that the Covenanters espoused when they allied themselves with the English Parliament in 1643 had been frustrated by the events of the past four years. They had gained security from Royalists, but an army of sectaries would soon gain power in

England, giving them renewed cause for alarm. They had been unable to mediate between king and Parliament, thereby providing another example to the axiom which promises woe to every would-be peacemaker. Finally, their dream of a truly Presbyterian England in close association with their own kirk failed to materialize. Yet failure is frequently relative, and the Scots did not realize in February 1647 how fortunate they actually were just to extricate themselves from the Civil War. It would take another foolhardy engagement, engineered in 1648 by the moderates, to teach them the disastrous consequences that invariably attend intervention in the affairs of another country, no matter how noble the motive.

NOTES

1. C.S.P.D., 1645, pp. 413, 575-576.
1. Meikle, pp. 128-129; D. Laing (ed.), *Correspondence of Sir Robert Kerr, First Earl of Ancram and His Son William, the Third Earl of Lothian,* 2 vols. (Edinburgh, 1875), I, pp. 181-182.
3. Charles L. Hamilton, "Anglo-Scottish Militia Negotiations," *Scottish History Review,* XLII (1963), pp. 86-88.
4. *Constitutional Documents,* pp. 290-306.
5. *Clarendon State Papers,* II, p. 243.
6. Montereul, I, p. 299.
7. C.J., IV, p. 686.
8. Baillie later recalled how Holles and Stapleton gave the Scots assurances that their early departure "was the only means to get that evil army disbanded, the King and peace settled to our minds" (III, p. 16).
9. Meikle, pp. 205-206.
10. Guthry, pp. 231-232; T. McCrie (ed.), *Life of Robert Blair* (Edinburgh, 1848), p. 193.
11. A. Peterkin (ed.), *Records of the Kirk of Scotland* (Edinburgh, 1838), pp. 489-490.
12. Burnet, *Hamilton,* p. 306.
13. *Clarendon State Papers,* MSS, Bodleian, 29, fol. 161.
14. *Acts and Ordinances,* I, pp. 907-908.
15. Montereul, I, p. 379; *Clarendon State Papers,* MSS, fol. 161v.
16. S. R. Gardiner, ed., *The Hamilton Papers* (London, 1880), pp. 120, 123-124.
17. *Parliament of Scotland,* VI, pp. 635-636.
18. C.J., V, P. 27; Burnet, *Hamilton,* p. 309.
19. Burnet, *Hamilton,* pp. 310-311.

20. *Parliament of Scotland,* VI, pp. 659-660.
21. Burnet, *Hamilton,* p. 311.
22. Guthry, pp. 237-238.
23. L.J., VIII, pp. 699, 716.
24. *Clarendon State Papers,* MSS, fol. 92.
25. A. F. Mitchell and J. Christie (eds.), *Records of the Commissioners of the General Assemblies* (Edinburgh, 1892), p. 75.

Abbreviations Used in Notes

(Full data for these materials and for citations in Notes appear in Bibliography.)

Acts and Ordinances: Acts and Ordinance of the Interregnum, 1642-1660.

Baillie: Robert Baillie, *Letters and Journal.*

Civil War: S. R. Gardiner, *History of the Great Civil War, 1642-1649.*

C.J.: *Journal of the House of Commons.*

Clarendon: Edward Hyde, Earl of Clarendon, *History of the Rebellion and the Civil Wars in England.*

Constitutional Documents: S. R. Gardiner, ed., *The Constitutional Documents of the Puritan Revolution.*

C.S.P.D.: *Calendar of State Papers, Domestic Series, The Reign of Charles I.*

C.S.P. Ven.: *Calendar of State Papers and Manuscripts Relating to English Affairs in the Archives of Venice, 1643-1647.*

Dewes: Sir Simonds Dewes, *Journal of the Parliament Begun November 3, 1640.*

D.N.B.: *Dictionary of National Biography.*

H.M.C.: *Reports of the Historical Manuscripts Commission.*

Instructions: Register of Instructions to the Scots Commissioners in London, 1644-1646.

L.J.: *Journal of the House of Lords.*

Manchester's Quarrel: Documents relating to the quarrel between the Earl of Manchester and Oliver Cromwell.

Sabran: *Negotiations de Monsieur de Sabran en Angleterre.*

T.T.: *Thomason Tracts.*

Yonge: Walter Yonge, *Journals of Proceedings in the House of Commons.*

Bibliography

PRIMARY SOURCES

A. Manuscripts

Carte MSS, Bodleian Library, Oxford, vol. 93.

Clarendon State Papers, MSS, Bodleian Library, vol. 29.

Dewes, Sir Simonds, *Journal of the Parliament Begun November 3, 1640,* British Museum, Harleian MSS, 164-166.

Hardwicke Papers, British Museum, MSS, 35, 838.

Harrington, John, *Parliamentary Diary,* British Museum, Add. MSS, 10, 114.

House of Lords Record Office, *Main Papers,* June 9, 1645-July 9, 1645.

Journal of the Common Council, Corporation of London Record Office, vol. 40.

Negotiations de Monsieur de Sabran en Angleterre, British Museum, Add.

MSS 5460-5461; Public Record Office, 31/3, vols. 74-82.

Register of Instructions to the Scots Commissioners in London, 1644-1646, General Register House, Edinburgh.

Whitacre, Laurence, *Diary of the Proceedings in the House of Commons,* British Museum, Add. MSS, 31, 116.

Whitelock, Bulstrode, *Annals,* British Museum, Add. MSS, 37, 343.

Wodrow MSS, LXV-LXVII, National Library of Scotland, Edinburgh.

Yonge, Walter, *Journals of Proceedings in the House of Commons,* British Museum, Add. MSS, 18,777-18,780.

B. Printed Material
Contemporary Pamphlets and Sermons

NOTE: Most of the pamphlets and sermons cited in this book are from the *Thomason Tracts,* and are referred to in the text by the number of the volume in the British Museum.

C. Newsbooks

Complete Intelligencer
Mercurius Aulicus
Mercurius Britanicus
Mercurius Civicus
Parliamentary Scout
Perfect Diurnall
Scottish Dove
Weekly Account

D. State Papers and Documents

Acts and Ordinances of the Interregnum, 1642-1660, ed. C. H. Firth and R. S. Rait, 3 vols., London, 1911.

Acts and Statutes of the Parliament of Scotland.

Calendar of State Papers, Domestic Series, the Reign of Charles I.

Calendar of State Papers and Manuscripts Relating to English Affairs in the Archives of Venice.

Collection of the State Papers of John Thurloe, 7 vols., 1742.

Constitutional Documents of the Puritan Revolution, 1625-1660, ed. S. R. Gardiner, Oxford, 1962.

Journal of the House of Commons.

Journal of the House of Lords.

Minutes of the Sessions of the Westminster Assembly of Divines, ed. A.F. Mitchell and J. Struthers, Edinburgh, 1874.

Records of the Commissioners of the General Assembly, ed. A. F. Mitchell and J. Christie, Edinburgh, 1892.

Records of the Kirk of Scotland, ed. Alexander Peterkin, Edinburgh, 1843.

Register of the Privy Council of Scotland, vol. II, Edinburgh, 1906.

Rushworth, John, *Historical Collections,* 7 vols., 1659-1701.

E. Private Correspondence, Diaries, Memoirs, and Other Contemporary Writings

Abbott, W. C. *Writings and Speeches of Oliver Cromwell,* vol. I. Cambridge, Mass., 1937.

Ashburnham, John. *A Narrative . . .,* 2 vols. London, 1830.

Baillie, Robert. *Letters and Journal,* ed. D. Laing, 3 vols. Edinburgh, 1841-1842.

Balfour, Sir James. *The Historical Works,* 4 vols. London, 1825.

Baxter, Richard. *Reliquiae Baxterianae.* London, 1696.

Bell, Robert (ed.). *The Correspondence of the Fairfax Family.* London, 1849.

Brereton, Sir William. *Travels.* Chatham Society, London, 1844.

Bruce, J. B. (ed.). *Charles I in 1646.* London, 1856.

Bruce, J. B. and Masson, D. (eds.). *Documents relating to the quarrel between the Earl of Manchester and Oliver Cromwell.* Camden Society, London, 1875.

Buchanan, David. *Truth Its Manifest.* London, 1645.

Burnet, Gilbert. *History of His Own Time,* 2 vols. London, 1724.

---. *The Memoirs of James and William, Dukes of Hamilton.* London, 1677.

Camden *Miscellany,* vol. VIII, 1883.

Carte, Thomas (ed.). *A Collection of Letters Written by Charles I,* 3 vols. London, 1735.

--- (ed.). *A Collection of Original Letters and Papers,* 2 vols. London, 1739.

Cary, H. (ed.). *Memorials of the Great Civil War,* 2 vols. London, 1842.

Dalrymple, D., Lord Hailes (eds.). *Memorials and Letters.* Glasgow, 1776.

Gardiner, S. R. (ed.). *The Hamilton Papers.* London, 1880.

Gillespie, George. *Notes and Debates and Proceedings of the Assembly of Divines.* Edinburgh, 1841.

Green, Mary (ed.). *Letters of Queen Henrietta Maria.* London, 1857.

Guthry, Henry. *Memoirs.* Glasgow, 1747.

Haller, William (ed.). *Tracts on Liberty in the Puritan Revolution,* 3 vols. New York, 1934.

Heylyn, Peter. *The History of the Presbyterians.* Oxford, 1670.

Hobbes, Thomas, "Behemoth," in F. Maseres (ed.), *Select Tracts.* London, 1815.

Holles, Denzil Lord. *Memoirs.* London, 1699.

Hyde, Edward, Earl of Clarendon. *The History of the Rebellion and the Civil Wars in England,* 6 vols. Oxford, 1888.

Lightfoot, John. "The Journals of the Assembly of Divines," *The Whole Works of the Rev. John Lightfoot,* ed. Rev. J. R. Pitman, 13 vols. London, 1825-1842.

Ludlow, Edmund. *Memoirs,* 2 vols. Oxford, 1894.

McCrie, T. (ed.). *Life of Robert Blair.* Edinburgh, 1848.

Meikle, H. W. (ed.). *Correspondence of the Scottish Commissioners in London.* London, 1917.

Montereul, Jean de. *The Diplomatic Correspondence,* 2 vols. Edinburgh, 1898.

Napier, Mark. *Memoirs of the Marquis of Montrose,* 2 vols. Edinburgh, 1856.

Nickolls, J. (ed.). *Original Letters and Papers Addressed to Oliver Cromwell.* London, 1743.

Peck, Francis. *Desiderata Curiosa.* London, 1779.

Reports of the Historical Manuscripts Commission:

MSS of the Duke of Hamilton

MSS of David Laing

MSS of the House of Lords

MSS of the Earl of Manchester

MSS of the Duke of Portland

MSS of Sir Henry Verney

Spalding, John. *The History of Troubles in Scotland,* 2 vols. Edinburgh, 1792.

Terry, Charles S. (ed.). *Papers Relating to the Army of the Solemn League and Covenant.* Edinburgh, 1917.

Turner, Sir James. *Memoirs of His Own Time.* Edinburgh, 1829.

Waller, Sir William. *Recollections.* London, 1788.

---. *Vindications of the Conduct and Character.* London, 1793.

Warriston, Archibald. *Diary.* Edinburgh, 1911.

Whitelock, Bulstrode. *Memorials of English Affairs,* 4 vols. London, 1853.

Wishart, George. *A Complete History of the Wars in Scotland.* Edinburgh, 1720.

Woodhouse, A. S. P. (ed.). *Puritanism and Liberty.* Chicago, 1951.

SECONDARY SOURCES

A. Books and Articles

Aylmer, G. E., "Place Bills and the Separation of Powers," *Transactions of the Royal Historical Society,* fifth series, vol. XV (1965), pp. 45-69.

Brunton, D. and Pennington, D. H. *Members of the Long Parliament.* London, 1954.

Burrell, Sidney A. "Calvinism, Capitalism and the Middle Classes," *Journal of Modern History,* vol. XXXII (1960), pp. 129-141.

Carruthers, S. W. *Everyday Work of the Westminster Assembly.* Philadelphia, 1943.

Chambers, Robert. *A Biographical Dictionary of Eminent Statesmen,* 4 vols. Glasgow, 1835.

Firth, C. H. *Cromwell's Army.* London, 1902.

---. *Oliver Cromwell.* London, 1961.

Gardiner, S. R. *History of England from the Accession of James I to the Outbreak of the Civil War,* 10 vols. London, 1896.

---. *History of the Great Civil War, 1642-1649,* 4 vols. London, 1893.

Haller, William. *Liberty and Reformation in the Puritan Revolution.* New York, 1955.

Hamilton, Charles L., "Anglo-Scottish Militia Negotiations," *Scottish History Review,* XLII (1963), pp. 86-88.

Hexter, J. H. *Reappraisals in History.* Aberdeen, 1962.

---. *The Reign of King Pym.* Cambridge, Mass., 1941.

Hill, Christopher. *God's Englishman.* New York, 1970.

Holmes, Clive. *The Eastern Association in the English Civil War.* Cambridge, England, 1974.

Kaplan, Lawrence, "The 'Plot' to Depose Charles I in 1644," *Bulletin of the Institute of Historical Research,* vol. XLIV (1971), pp. 216-223.

---. "Presbyterians and Independents in 1643," *English Historical Review,* vol. LXXXIV (1969), pp. 244-256.

---, "Steps to War: The Scots and Parliament, 1642-1643," *Journal of British Studies,* vol. IX (May 1970), pp. 50-70.

Kershaw, R. N., "The Recruiting of the Long Parliament," *History,* vol. VIII (1923).

Liu, Tai. *Discord in Zion: The Puritan Divines and the Puritan Revolution.* The Hague, 1973.

MacCormack, John R. *Revolutionary Politics in the Long Parliament.* Cambridge, Mass., 1973.

MacKenzie, W. C. *The Life and Times of John Maitland.* London, 1902.

Mathieson, William. *Politics and Religion,* 2 vols. Glasgow, 1902.

Miller, Perry. *Orthodoxy in Massachusetts.* Boston, 1959.

Mulligan, Lotte (Glow), "Pym and Parliament, the Methods of Moderation," *Journal of Modern History* (1964), pp. 373-97.

--- (Glow), "The Scottish Alliance and the Committee of Both Kingdoms," *Historical Studies,* vol. XIV (1970), pp. 173-88.

Notestein, Wallace, "The Establishment of the Committee of Both Kingdoms," *American Historical Review,* vol. XVII (1912), pp. 477-495.

Peace, T. C. *The Leveller Movement.* Baltimore, 1916.

Pearl, Valerie, "London's Counter Revolution," in G. E. Aylmer (ed.), *The Interregnum: The Quest for Settlement.* London, 1972, pp. 29-56.

---, "London Puritans and Scotch Fifth Columnists," in A. E. J. Hollaender and W. Kellaway (eds.), *Essays in London History Presented to Philip Edmund Jones.* London, 1969, pp. 317-331.

---, "Oliver St. John and the 'Middle Group' in the Long Parliament," *English Historical Review,* vol. LXXXI (1966), pp. 490-519.

---, "The Royal Independents' in the English Civil War," *Transactions of the Royal Historical Society,* fifth series, vol. XVIII (1968), pp. 69-96.

Rowe, Violet A. *Sir Henry Vane, the Younger.* London, 1970.

Shaw, W. A. *History of the English Church During the Civil Wars and Under the Protectorate.* London, 1900.

Snow, Vernon. *Essex, the Rebel.* Lincoln, Neb., 1970.

Stevenson, David, "The Financing of the Cause of the Covenanters, 1638-51," *Scottish History Review,* vol. LI (1972), pp. 89-123.

---, "The Radical Party in the Kirk, 1637-45," *Journal of Ecclesiastical History,* vol. XXV (1974), pp. 135-65.

---. *The Scottish Revolution, 1637-44.* Newton Abbott, 1973.

Trevor-Roper, H. R. *Archbishop Laud.* London, 1962.

---, "Fast Sermons of the Long Parliament," *Essays in British History Presented to Sir Keith Feiling.* London, 1964.

---, "Scotland and the Puritan Revolution," *Historical Essays Presented to David Ogg.* London, 1963.

Underdown, David, "The Independents Reconsidered," *Journal of British Studies,* vol. III (1964), pp. 57-84.

---, "Party Management in the Recruiter Elections, 1645-48," *English*

Historical Review, vol. 83 (1968), pp. 235-264.

Wedgwood, C. V., "The Elector Palatine and the Civil War," *History Today,* vol. IV (1954), pp. 3-10.

---. *The King's Peace.* London, 1955.

---. *The King's War.* London, 1958.

---. *Montrose.* London, 1958.

---. *Thomas Wentworth, First Earl of Strafford.* London, 1962.

Wilson, John F. *Pulpit in Parliament.* Princeton, 1969.

B. Unpublished Theses

Bigby, D. A., "The Relations between England and France during the Great Rebellion," M.A. thesis, London University, 1912.

Buchanan, John N., "Charles I and the Scots," Ph.D. thesis, University of Toronto, 1965.

Hamilton, Charles Louis, "The Covenanters and Parliament, 1640-46," Ph.D. thesis, Cornell University, 1959.

Hexter, J. H., "The Rise of the Independent Party," Ph.D. thesis, Harvard University, 1936.

Williams, C. M., "The Political Career of Henry Marten," D. Phil. thesis, Oxford University, 1954.

Index

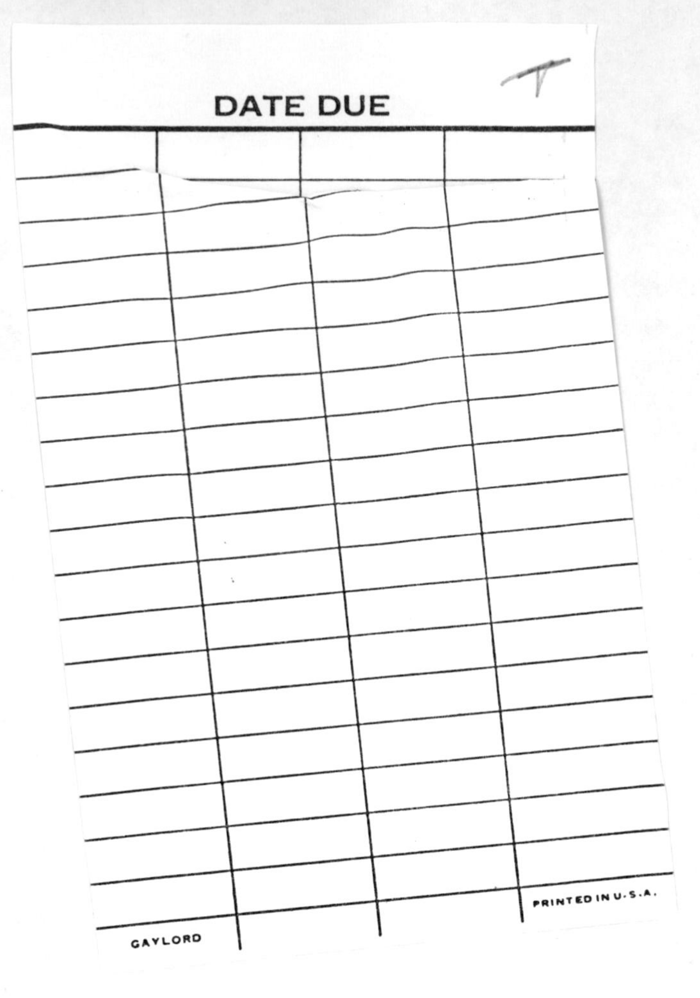
DATE DUE
GAYLORD
PRINTED IN U.S.A.